THE BEDFORD SERIES IN HISTORY AND CULTURE

The 1912 Election and the Power of Progressivism

A Brief History with Documents

Related Titles in
THE BEDFORD SERIES IN HISTORY AND CULTURE
Advisory Editors: Natalie Zemon Davis, Princeton University
Ernest R. May, Harvard University
Lynn Hunt, University of California, Los Angeles
David W. Blight, Yale University

---

*The Rebuilding of Old Commonwealths and Other Documents of Social
Reform in the Progressive Era South*
 Edited with an Introduction by William A. Link, *University of North
 Carolina at Greensboro*

Muckraking: Three Landmark Articles
 Edited with an Introduction by Ellen F. Fitzpatrick, *University of New
 Hampshire*

PLUNKITT OF TAMMANY HALL *by William L. Riordon*
 Edited with an Introduction by Terrence J. McDonald, *University of
 Michigan*

Talking Back to Civilization: Indian Voices from the Progressive Era
 Edited with an Introduction by Frederick E. Hoxie, *University of Illinois at
 Urbana–Champaign*

TWENTY YEARS AT HULL-HOUSE *by Jane Addams*
 Edited with an Introduction by Victoria Bissell Brown, *Grinnell College*

Muller v. Oregon: A Brief History with Documents
 Nancy Woloch, *Barnard College*

OTHER PEOPLE'S MONEY AND HOW THE BANKERS USE IT *by Louis D.
Brandeis*
 Edited with an Introduction by Melvin I. Urofsky, *Virginia Commonwealth
 University*

THE BEDFORD SERIES IN HISTORY AND CULTURE

The 1912 Election and the Power of Progressivism

A Brief History with Documents

Brett Flehinger

California State University, San Bernardino

BEDFORD/ST. MARTIN'S   Boston ♦ New York

For Bedford/St. Martin's

Publisher for History: Patricia A. Rossi
Director of Development for History: Jane Knetzger
Developmental Editor: Molly E. Kalkstein
Editorial Assistant, Publishing Services: Maria Teresa Burwell
Senior Production Supervisor: Tina Cameron
Marketing Manager: Jenna Bookin Barry
Project Management: Books By Design, Inc.
Text Design: Claire Seng-Niemoeller
Indexer: Books By Design, Inc.
Cover Design: Billy Boardman
Cover Photos: William Taft Campaigns from a Train © Bettmann/CORBIS; *President Woodrow Wilson Delivering Speech* © CORBIS; *Theodore Roosevelt on Campaign Trail* © CORBIS; *Eugene Debs,* Photo courtesy of The Eugene V. Debs Foundation, Terre Haute, Indiana.
Composition: Stratford Publishing Services, Inc.
Printing and Binding: Haddon Craftsmen, an RR Donnelley & Sons Company

President: Joan E. Feinberg
Editorial Director: Denise B. Wydra
Director of Marketing: Karen R. Melton
Director of Editing, Design, and Production: Marcia Cohen
Manager, Publishing Services: Emily Berleth

Library of Congress Control Number: 2002106597

For information, write: Bedford/St. Martin's, 75 Arlington Street, Boston, MA 02116 (617-399-4000)

ISBN: 0-312-26029-6

Acknowledgments

Acknowledgments and copyrights appear at the back of the book on page 193, which constitutes an extension of the copyright page.

Foreword

The Bedford Series in History and Culture is designed so that readers can study the past as historians do.

The historian's first task is finding the evidence. Documents, letters, memoirs, interviews, pictures, movies, novels, or poems can provide facts and clues. Then the historian questions and compares the sources. There is more to do than in a courtroom, for hearsay evidence is welcome, and the historian is usually looking for answers beyond act and motive. Different views of an event may be as important as a single verdict. How a story is told may yield as much information as what it says.

Along the way the historian seeks help from other historians and perhaps from specialists in other disciplines. Finally, it is time to write, to decide on an interpretation and how to arrange the evidence for readers.

Each book in this series contains an important historical document or group of documents, each document a witness from the past and open to interpretation in different ways. The documents are combined with some element of historical narrative—an introduction or a biographical essay, for example—that provides students with an analysis of the primary source material and important background information about the world in which it was produced.

Each book in the series focuses on a specific topic within a specific historical period. Each provides a basis for lively thought and discussion about several aspects of the topic and the historian's role. Each is short enough (and inexpensive enough) to be a reasonable one-week assignment in a college course. Whether as classroom or personal reading, each book in the series provides firsthand experience of the challenge—and fun—of discovering, recreating, and interpreting the past.

Natalie Zemon Davis
Ernest R. May
Lynn Hunt
David W. Blight

Preface

The 1912 presidential election was a unique moment in the Progressive Era because it drew together politicians, social reformers, intellectuals, and economists onto a single stage and produced a many-sided national debate about the future of America's economic, political, and social structure. This book was shaped by the idea that elections can take the form of public conversations, and that focusing on the participants and the central issue in the 1912 election can draw students into Progressivism and help them draw together the "tissues" of progressive reform.

This volume explores the political-economic ideas of Progressivism and the 1912 election while focusing on two interrelated themes. First, many of the documents in this collection focus on the rise of corporate power (the "trust problem"), which was the central issue of the Progressive Era as well as the election. Corporate concentration became the dominant issue in 1912 because of its broad influence on social and political life in early-twentieth-century America, and all of the presidential candidates understood that organized wealth and business combinations were a pressing economic problem that had clear social and political effects outside the world of commerce. Second, in the views of almost all participants in the election, monopoly was both a product of the breakdown of democracy and a sign that key American political institutions were in desperate need of reform. Democratic candidate Woodrow Wilson depicted an octopus-like menace, stating, "the tentacles of these things [corporations] spread in every direction, and until we have broken their inside control, the government is helpless to assist the people." Progressives saw a fundamental connection between political structures and social and economic conditions, and, simply stated, they hoped political innovation would produce a more equitable society, which was their primary concern. Students reading this volume will see that although Progressivism fought its battles in political contests, the courts, and legislatures, the solutions proposed by each candidate went to the heart of American social and economic life.

To help students get a feeling for the people and issues critical to understanding Progressivism and the 1912 election, part one of this volume is an introduction, "The Story of 1912: 'A Year Supreme with Possibilities.'" The first chapter in part one, "'Progressive': The Popular Label," introduces all of the 1912 candidates, places the reader in the middle of the chaos the Republicans faced, and explores the reasons for the Democrats' confidence, while Socialist candidate Eugene V. Debs waited for his moment. The next chapter, "The Problem of the Progressive Era," brings alive the issues of the 1912 election, in particular the problem of corporate capitalism. The final chapter in part one, aptly titled "The Candidates Debate," brings together the candidates described in the first part with the issues examined in the second. Part one ends with a brief discussion of how this important election has influenced American politics right up to the present.

Part two, "The Documents," does not attempt to include documents from all of the figures who could be considered Progressives. Instead, through speeches, letters, articles, and political cartoons, it aims for deep coverage of the central figures in the 1912 election to allow students to see both the complexity of the issues and how reformers' ideas developed over time and through interaction with competing programs for reform. Each chapter in part two focuses on one of the four presidential candidates. Chapter 4 includes substantial selections from three of Theodore Roosevelt's most important speeches as well as letters to and from Roosevelt's advisers to show how outside pressure, in this case from middle-class female reformers, shaped Roosevelt's democratic and economic reforms. Other documents in chapter 4 and chapter 5 show Louis Brandeis as an intermediary between failed Republican candidate Robert La Follette and Woodrow Wilson. Collectively, these three reformers developed a program to restrain corporate growth that was greater than any of their individual ideas. Finally, the documents in chapters 6 and 7 highlight the critical roles both William Howard Taft and Eugene Debs played in the election as well. Taft's letters and speeches show his very real concern for the impact of Roosevelt's ideas on traditional American constitutional liberties, whereas Debs's ideas show the limits of the other candidates' ideas and the fundamental difference between reform and radicalism. The picture that emerges from the documents is not a simple two-sided debate of the merits of New Nationalism versus New Freedom, but a complex conversation. And in their depth the documents clearly demonstrate that there was no single strand of Progressivism—that, in fact, Progressivism was a broad movement created by the competing and intersecting ideas of early-twentieth-century reformers.

Some of the candidates' speeches in the 1912 election influenced not only how the nation perceived itself but also the future course of events. Speeches by today's presidential candidates do not often pack this kind of punch. The letters of the 1912 candidates and their constituents offer an insider's look at just how much the candidates needed to know before they could make these speeches. And the political cartoons offer an important and amusing portrayal of how Americans reacted to the speeches and buzzwords of the candidates they were getting to know. This volume would not be complete without these speeches, the letters that helped the candidates write their speeches, and the reactions to them. Headnotes, allowing students to conduct a critical reading of the documents, precede each document. A chronology of the Progressive Era, questions for consideration, and an annotated bibliography conclude the book.

ACKNOWLEDGMENTS

As series adviser and my graduate adviser, Ernest May provided encouragement and support for this project throughout the process. Bedford/St. Martin's History Publisher Patricia Rossi has been supportive and patient as the book has come together. Others at Bedford/ St. Martin's who helped make this book possible include Emily Berleth, Billy Boardman, and Jane Knetzger. Developmental Editor Molly Kalkstein played a crucial role in this volume. Her editorial skill has made this a far clearer and better book than it would have been without her. Furthermore, as I moved from Massachusetts to California in the midst of this project, her organizational abilities helped hold this project together despite geographical confusion.

This volume was also improved by the careful attention of a number of academic reviewers, and I am grateful for their assistance. John Buenker of the University of Wisconsin–Parkside, John Milton Cooper Jr. of the University of Wisconsin–Madison, Michael Green of the Community College of Southern Nevada, Michael Kazin of Georgetown University, Eric Rauchway of the University of California at Davis, Nancy Unger of Santa Clara University, and one anonymous reviewer all provided helpful suggestions and critiques that significantly improved this book.

No one can make it through putting a book together, or the academic world, without building up important friendships. Dani Botsman, Cathy Corman, Joyce Hanson, Arthur Hock, Ward McAfee, Jon Rosenberg, Kent Schofield, Jerry Sweeney, and Tom Underwood have all brightened my life, and I appreciate the good fortune I've had in gaining their friendship. My greatest thanks go to my family. My two children, Andrew and Cameron, remind me that although it is great fun to think about the past, the future is worth a good deal of my attention as well. Suzanne Lane, my wife, in addition to being an outstanding scholar in her own right and an invaluable editor and critic, has brightened my life in ways that go far beyond the limits of any single volume. This book is dedicated to Suzanne, Andrew, and Cameron with love.

Brett Flehinger

Contents

THE BEDFORD SERIES IN HISTORY AND CULTURE

The 1912 Election and the Power of Progressivism

A Brief History with Documents

PART ONE

Introduction:
The Story of 1912:
"A Year Supreme
with Possibilities"

1

"Progressive": The Popular Label

"Nineteen twelve," wrote Socialist party presidential candidate Eugene V. Debs, "is a year supreme with possibilities."[1] Although Debs hoped to inspire his rising band of radicals and labor activists in particular, his words also apply more broadly to the election as a whole. Rarely have American voters faced as wide an array of choices as they did in 1912. The ballot listed three men who had been, or would be, elected president of the United States: William Howard Taft, the Republican incumbent; Theodore Roosevelt, Taft's predecessor, who had left the Republican party to form the new Progressive party; and Woodrow Wilson, a Democrat and the ultimate victor in 1912. And if this were not enough, having won elections in cities across the United States, the Socialist party and its nominee, Debs, looked forward to the election with greater confidence than ever before.

With four nationally recognized candidates in the race (Debs, Roosevelt, Taft, and Wilson) as well as hotly contested nominating conventions for both the Republicans and Democrats, the 1912 campaign was a remarkable spectacle. The long friendship of Theodore Roosevelt and William Howard Taft unraveled as Roosevelt publicly denounced Taft as incompetent and a "fathead." Taft shot back, calling Roosevelt a demagogue and a dictator with a Messiah complex.[2] Furthermore, the chaos spread beyond the political arena. Taft suffered two debilitating losses during the campaign. In April 1912, one of his leading advisors, Archie Butt, died in the sinking of the *Titanic*.[3] Then, just days before the election, Taft's running mate, James Sherman, died following an extended illness. Roosevelt narrowly avoided a similar fate. In Milwaukee, Wisconsin, an assassin shot him in the chest; then, despite advice from his friends and doctors to go to the hospital, Roosevelt delivered his speech before consenting to surgery. Even Woodrow Wilson, the ultimate victor, did not emerge from the campaign unscathed. Just two days before the election, Wilson's car hit a bump in the road, throwing the presidential candidate against the

3

roof and opening up a four-inch cut in his scalp. In any other campaign such an injury would have been big news, but in 1912 it was a minor incident in a two-year melodrama.

The election of 1912, however, was far more than a series of dramatic moments. In the fall of 1912, as the campaign reached its final stages, a *Chicago Daily News* political cartoonist captured the central theme of the campaign. The cartoon showed all of the candidates rushing into a store advertising "Progressive Underwear for the Coming Fall." (See Document 36.) In the foreground the rotund and conservative William Howard Taft charges in, hoping that the store will have "anything big enough for me." Taft is not disappointed because on the shelf is a box labeled "Progressive Standpatter" (a nickname for conservative or "regular" Republicans). While Taft finds his underwear, the Democratic nominee Woodrow Wilson tries on a pair of "Progressive Democratic Brand" underwear and tells Taft, "I've always worn 'em, Bill, and they don't scratch a bit." The minor candidates are also pictured: Debs, the Socialist party candidate, opens a box of "Progressive Socialist" underwear, while Prohibition party* candidate Eugene Chafin comes out of the back room with a "Progressive Prohibition" undershirt. Interestingly, Roosevelt is the only candidate not pictured in the store. Roosevelt was running on the Progressive party ticket, and as a self-proclaimed Progressive. He could safely be assumed to wear Progressive underwear and had presumably purchased his long before they became popular.

As well as giving an amusing introduction to most of the candidates, this cartoon highlights the importance of the 1912 election. No single leader dominated Progressivism, and different reformers could make it fit their own distinctive needs. Nevertheless, at its core, Progressivism was the attempt to use government and new private quasi-governmental institutions to help America's political and social system adjust to a series of economic changes that took place between the 1870s and 1920. Although the candidates in the 1912 election differed on how best to reform America, they fundamentally agreed on the need for reform. Like shoppers following a fad, all of the candidates tried to claim the "progressive" label as their own, and at its most

---

*The Prohibition party was a single-interest party representing anti-alcohol activists. Although it fielded presidential candidates in every election between 1892 and 1916, the party never gained more than 2 percent of the popular vote. Nonetheless, Chafin's inclusion in the cartoon shows the extent to which the Progressive label could be claimed by any- and everyone.

basic level the election of 1912 was a fight for control of the progressive reform movement.[4]

At one time or another all four of the candidates in the race laid claim to being the one true reformer and leader of the decade-long progressive reform movement. Roosevelt staked the first and most direct claim to the progressive label. He challenged Taft for the Republican party presidential nomination, arguing that Taft had betrayed the reform foundation that Roosevelt had built between 1901 and 1909. Unable to defeat Taft, Roosevelt continued to claim to be the true progressive, breaking from the Republicans and starting a third party, named the Progressive party.[5] Taft, however, was not willing to concede so easily and pointed to his record of political, economic, and social reforms, asking "whether I am not entitled to the same name of progressive as a great many people who have been going around talking about progressives and never doing anything."[6] Wilson, a Democrat, had his own claim as a reformer. In 1910 he had been president of Princeton University and then had quickly been elected governor of New Jersey before winning the Democratic presidential nomination in 1912. This rapid rise from academia to political leadership cast him as an outsider and a disinterested expert who could reform a corrupt political and economic system. Even Debs, who criticized progressive reforms as feeble attempts to prop up capitalism and lumped all three parties together as "capitalist" parties, claimed the progressive label, stating "the really progressive planks in the Progressive platform were taken bodily from the Socialist platform."[7]

Republican Chaos

In practical terms, the controversies of 1912 developed out of the two previous presidential elections. The night he won the presidency in his own right in 1904, Roosevelt declared that he would not accept renomination or election in 1908. Immensely popular and in control of the Republican party, Roosevelt was in the rare position of being able to name his successor when his term came to an end. Although Republican reformers such as Wisconsin's Robert M. La Follette and Iowa's Albert Cummins* had gained power by attacking Republican conservatives during Roosevelt's time in office, few expected

---

*La Follette had served as Wisconsin's governor from 1900 to 1905 and then entered the U.S. Senate. Cummins followed a similar pattern, first winning election as governor in 1901 and then moving on to the Senate in 1907.

Roosevelt to choose one of the new insurgents.[8] Indeed, he steered a middle-of-the-road course and selected his secretary of war, William Howard Taft, a well-respected but uninspiring choice who was also unlikely to offend most party members. Although few Republicans challenged Taft for the nomination, Roosevelt commanded the loyalty of most party members, and with Roosevelt's influence Taft secured the Republican nomination and defeated the Democratic candidate, William Jennings Bryan, in the general election.

The Trouble with Taft

As Roosevelt left office he explained why he had selected Taft, writing, "I have the profound satisfaction of knowing that he [Taft] will do all in his power to further every one of the great causes for which I have fought and that he will persevere in every one of the great governmental policies in which I most firmly believe."[9] Furthering Roosevelt's "great causes" and persevering in his "great governmental policies," however, would prove to be a difficult task. Simply following Roosevelt, who had redefined the presidency as an activist's "bully pulpit," meant that the less energetic Taft was likely to pale in comparison. Furthermore, in stepping out of Roosevelt's shadow and defining his own presidency, Taft alienated many of Roosevelt's staunch supporters. On the other hand, simply acting like Roosevelt would have reinforced the idea that Taft had not won the office on his own, and he would have appeared to be Roosevelt's puppet.

Even as he assumed office, Taft was forced to contend with multiple divisions in his own party, further complicating the task he faced as president. By 1908 there had been a split in the Republican party between a dominant, older, conservative, generally eastern wing oriented toward business and finance that had controlled the party since the 1890s, and an increasingly aggressive group of insurgent Republicans who had gained control of midwestern and western Republican organizations by attacking conservative Republicans as aggressively as they went after Democrats.* Wisconsin's three-term governor, Robert La Follette, was one of the leading Republican reformers. He had gained power by exposing the political and ethical failures of his

---

*Conservative Republicans were often referred to as the "old guard" in recognition of their longtime control of the Republican party. The new generation of Republicans were initially called "insurgents" because they attempted to reform the party by working from within. By 1910 they had come to be known as "Progressives."

fellow party members in Wisconsin, and when he entered the Senate he threatened to continue this strategy nationwide.[10]

As president, Roosevelt had used this tension to his advantage, operating as both a national spokesperson for the new progressive movement and a liaison to the conservative wing, thereby holding the party together and increasing his power. Few politicians, however, had the skill to carry out such a balancing act, and although an able administrator, Taft was entirely out of his depth. In choosing his cabinet, Taft selected more corporate lawyers than professional politicians. Although his reasoning (that corporations could afford to hire the best legal minds, and therefore he would draw from the same pool) may have been intellectually sound, his actions were politically naïve. His choices angered the reformers in his party who were trying to restrain many of the corporations that had formerly employed Taft's cabinet members, and the reformers believed that corporate lawyers would be unlikely to rule with the broad public interest in mind.[11] Finally, when Taft refused to support the reformers' attempt to depose House Speaker Joseph Cannon,* one of the symbols and leaders of the old guard Republicans, he alienated one wing of his party in his first days in office.[12]

Angering the insurgents wasn't catastrophic because these vociferous dissenters were a minority in the party, and Taft knew that until they could depose the old guard he could ill afford to alienate the party's ruling congressional leaders. However, when he further alienated Roosevelt's loyalists, Taft seriously weakened his position in the party. His choices for cabinet members angered many of those closest to Roosevelt, not because of whom he chose, but simply because he was changing the cabinet at all. As Henry Cabot Lodge,† a conservative Republican senator from Massachusetts and one of Roosevelt's close friends, complained, "it was evidently the intention to get rid of every person who might keep Taft in touch with the Roosevelt influence."[13] Worse still for Taft, in 1909 one of his appointees, Secretary of Interior Richard Achilles Ballinger, clashed over conservation policy

---

*Joseph Cannon was a Republican member of Congress from Illinois whose aggressive use of his power as speaker of the House of Representatives came to be seen by many Republican reformers as a symbol of conservative mismanagement of government. In 1909 Taft initially supported the attempt of progressive Republican members of Congress to force Cannon out, but when other conservatives threatened to block his legislative agenda, Taft withdrew his support for the reformers.

†Lodge was a U.S. Senator from Massachusetts and although he was considerably more conservative than Roosevelt, both men came from similarly privileged backgrounds, which included attending Harvard University.

with Chief Forester Gifford Pinchot, a holdover from Roosevelt's years in office and one of the former president's connections to the insurgents. When Taft sided with Ballinger the insurgents and Roosevelt supporters came together in an anti-Taft alliance.[14]

The legislative situation in Congress reinforced the challenge Taft faced in holding his party together. In 1912 most federal revenue was raised through a tariff—a tax on consumption by which Congress set rates, or duties, for both raw materials and manufactured goods imported into the United States. Although used to raise federal revenue, tariffs also shaped the economy. Prohibitively high rates closed off imports, allowing U.S. manufacturers to develop their products without the threat of foreign challengers, but at the cost of higher prices for consumers. Lower rates exposed U.S. manufacturers and producers to foreign competition but helped consumers by lowering prices. Consequently, the tariff indirectly affected almost every economic constituency in one way or another, and it was the most volatile issue of late-nineteenth-century U.S. politics.

The tariff also marked a major division between the two major parties and the different sections of the country. The Republicans had built their party by using the tariff to favor special interest groups who provided loyal support. Republicans believed in protecting industry and labor, and argued that duties should be set high enough to compensate for low labor costs in other countries and to provide a favorable market for U.S. manufacturers.[15] Democrats, on the other hand, tended to favor limited tariffs, arguing that Congress should set rates only as necessary to raise funds, and had used their opposition to the tariff to appeal to key Democratic voting blocks, particularly the agricultural South.

As president, Roosevelt had simply avoided the tariff issue altogether. When Taft took over in 1909, the tariff laws, more than a decade old, required revision. To his credit, Taft addressed the situation directly, declaring himself a "tariff revisionist."[16] Such directness, however, paid him few political dividends. It brought him into the fight between insurgent Republicans who wanted to lower rates on manufactured goods in order to benefit consumers, and their conservative counterparts, who favored keeping tariffs high.[17] When Rhode Island senator Nelson Aldrich* blatantly disregarded the insurgents and

---

*Aldrich was a U.S. senator from Rhode Island, and the most powerful Republican in the Senate. A multimillionaire and related by marriage to the Rockefeller family, Aldrich saw politics from the point of view of business and industrial leaders.

rammed through a bill that provided for limited reductions, Taft came under pressure to veto it. Unwilling to begin his administration by crossing the strongest Republicans in Congress, however, Taft signed the bill into law. Taft's signing of the bill merely angered many reform-minded midwestern Republicans, but his attempts to explain his actions caused them to revolt. In a series of speeches in 1909 Taft lauded Aldrich, the man the insurgents hated most, as "the real leader in the Senate," and then, while appearing in the district of James Tawney, the one midwestern Republican who had supported the tariff, Taft publicly claimed that the new bill was "the best tariff bill that the Republican Party ever passed."[18] By stating this directly in the upper Midwest—the heartland of the Republican insurgents—Taft had transformed a private party disagreement into a public struggle for control of the Republican party.

Tensions between Taft and the insurgents deepened as more of the president's legislative agenda came through Congress. When Attorney General George Wickersham supported a bill to alter the operation of the Interstate Commerce Commission,* the nation's oldest regulatory body, the insurgents attacked with hundreds of amendments. This challenge forced Taft's legislative allies to rewrite the bill, expanding federal regulation enough that the insurgents ultimately voted to pass it. By 1910 Taft had turned against the reformers, demanding that "disloyal" members be cast out of the Republican party. Less than two years into his presidency, Taft was in a legislative and political war with the reformers in his party.[19] Furthermore, he appeared to have sided with the old guard and to have repudiated the claim to be Roosevelt's successor.

With the insurgents in open revolt there was little doubt that at least one reformer would challenge Taft for the presidential nomination in 1912. In early 1911, nine dissident Republican senators, thirteen members of the House of Representatives, six governors, and a number of party activists came together to create the National Progressive Republican League (NPRL)—an alternative to Taft's control of the Republican party. Although nominally formed to promote "popular government and progressive legislation," the NPRL's main mission was to oppose Taft in the election of 1912, and by the late spring of 1911, Wisconsin senator Robert La Follette, the Republican reformer

---

*Created by Congress in 1887, the Interstate Commerce Commission was a federal regulatory agency that had limited influence over interstate railroad rates.

with the highest national profile, announced that he would challenge Taft for the party's presidential nomination.[20]

"My Hat Is in the Ring": Roosevelt Returns

Roosevelt returned from an African safari in 1910 believing that under Taft "the Republican Party consists of leadership which has no following."[21] He tried to reclaim his role maintaining balance in the party, but because he was no longer president he could not command the loyalty that kept the peace. Furthermore, the party that he returned to in 1910 was significantly more divided than it had been two years earlier, and although Roosevelt tried to pacify both sides, he was quickly put in a position of having to support one faction or the other. Within months of returning in 1910, Roosevelt reentered party politics, serving as a delegate to a badly divided New York State Republican convention. Later in the year, he went on a high-profile speaking tour during which he presented his new outline for America's political and economic development—the New Nationalism. (See Document 1.) Although Roosevelt's speeches seemed to place him in the insurgents' camp, by the campaign season he had moved to the middle and was speaking in support of Republican insurgent and conservative candidates. Roosevelt, however, had practical reasons for this split.[22] Although he agreed with the insurgents and privately derided Taft as a "flubdub with a streak of the second rate and the common in him," he resisted publicly opposing Taft, whom he considered unbeatable for renomination in 1912.[23] (See also Document 3.)

Despite Roosevelt's best efforts the split in the party widened, and as it did he became the focus of attention. Both Taft and his opposition attempted to gain Roosevelt's endorsement. Aside from the political value that Roosevelt could offer, both sides also had a greater fear: Roosevelt's reentry into presidential politics. In 1910 Roosevelt was only fifty-two years old and still the most popular politician in the country. Although he denied having any political ambitions, many believed he wanted to return to the White House—a belief that only grew stronger when he refused to rule out the possibility.

As early as 1910, Roosevelt had advised his supporters that he did not want the nomination, and the reason he gave was telling: He predicted a Democratic victory in 1912 and concluded, "For every reason I most earnestly hope the conservatives will retain sufficient control to make Taft's nomination inevitable."[24] From this point on, Roosevelt denied interest in the nomination, but he had also worked to protect his availability. When correspondents asked him to publicly state his unwillingness to run, he claimed that he did not want the nomination, but would not be forced into limiting his options. Given his popularity, profile, and de facto reentry into politics, Roosevelt remained the focus of attention simply by refusing to refuse to enter the race.

In denying his interest, Roosevelt provided guidelines for how he might accept the nomination. He commented that if the public demanded that he enter the race, it would be dishonorable not to answer the people's call. In his letter to Michigan's governor Chase Osborn (Document 3), however, Roosevelt carefully outlined the way to create such an overwhelming demand that he would feel duty bound to accept: "The letter to me might briefly state the writer's belief that the people of his State, or their states, desire to have me run for the presidency, and to know whether in such a case I would refuse the nomination." (For a different view of Osborn, see Taft's reference to "the lunatic governor out there [Michigan]" in Document 32.) Although he wrote to a fellow Republican party leader to solicit his support, Roosevelt insisted that if it were clear "that the people as a whole desire me, not for my own sake, but for their sake, to undertake the job, I would be duty bound to do so."

Consequently, when La Follette, the Republican with the longest record of reform, began to campaign against Taft in the winter of 1911, he worried as much about defeating Roosevelt as he did Taft. Although well known, La Follette had little support outside his home state of Wisconsin. By January 1912, La Follette worried openly that a number of his campaign workers were preparing to shift their support to Roosevelt. In February 1912, La Follette, under pressure from the campaign and a family member's illness, provided the opportunity Roosevelt's supporters needed. In a speech in Philadelphia La Follette bumbled badly. He spoke for over two hours, lost track of his thoughts, verbally attacked his audience, and was rumored to have had a mental breakdown.[25] Despite his refusal to withdraw, rumors ran wild that La Follette would quit and offer his support to Roosevelt. Although La Follette remained in the race through the Republican convention, he was never again a major factor, winning fewer than one hundred delegates.

A few days after La Follette's disaster in Philadelphia, Roosevelt entered the campaign, stating, "My hat is in the ring."[26] After he entered the race, Roosevelt became the focus of the campaign. In a speech delivered a few days before he announced his entry into the race, Roosevelt outlined a plan for economic justice and renewed democracy (see Document 4) and attacked Taft openly and aggressively. Taft, in turn, was drawn into the campaign when he saw Roosevelt threatening both his nomination and the legalistic constitutionalism he believed in. (See Document 32.) Reluctantly, Taft fought back, going on a speaking tour of crucial Republican states. (See Documents 30, 31, and 33.) At this point the campaign became particularly nasty. Roosevelt stated that Taft was antidemocratic, beholden to corrupt bosses, and a turncoat who had betrayed the Roosevelt legacy. Taft refuted Roosevelt's points and painted his former friend as a power-hungry, would-be dictator, who might never give up office if reelected.

Democracy Redefined: The Republican Nomination

Although the charges, responses, and name-calling that the candidates engaged in may have been spectacular to witness, the most critical events in determining the Republican nominee took place out of the public eye. For the first time in American history, voters in states such as North Dakota, Oregon, and Nebraska voted in direct primary elections for their party's presidential candidate. Roosevelt dominated the Republican primaries, winning a healthy majority of the delegates (the people who would actually select the nominee at the convention) chosen through popular election. Unfortunately for Roosevelt, 1912 marked the beginning of the transition to popular primaries, and the majority of delegates to the national convention—the people who would actually select the presidential nominee—were chosen in private meetings, called caucuses. Although Roosevelt was the most popular candidate, Taft controlled most of the delegations chosen through caucuses, where his ability to appoint loyal supporters to state party jobs helped him win this critical support.

Southern states* stood at the center of Taft's strategy; although Republicans stood little chance of winning the electoral votes of the ex-Confederate states, these states had sent numerous delegates to previous national Republican conventions, allowing national leaders to retain control of the party. Because southern Republican leaders had virtually no chance of winning elections against Democrats and gaining the patronage jobs that went with statewide office, they depended

---

*In the years after the end of Reconstruction, southern states had used legal and constitutional changes to deny most African American males the right to vote. Because African Americans were the most important group of Republican voters in the South, their disfranchisement left the South with one dominant political party, the Democrats, who were firmly associated with white supremacy.

solely on the national Republican party and its leadership for jobs and power. As the incumbent, Taft had either appointed many of the southern Republican officeholders, or had the power to dismiss them from their jobs, assuring the loyalty of the vast majority of southern Republican delegates. In 1910, seeing the coming challenge Taft had been sure to secure loyal delegations from the South; this organizational advantage and quick thinking provided him with the margin he needed to retain control of the Republican party and ensure his nomination. Ironically, Taft's strategy owed a great deal to Roosevelt's example. In 1908 Roosevelt had used the party machinery in the South to make sure that Taft gained the nomination. Although Taft is generally thought to have lacked Roosevelt's political skill, in 1912 he both matched and mastered Roosevelt.[27]

As Republicans met for their national convention in Chicago in June 1912, Taft held slightly more than the majority of delegates needed to nominate him for a second term. However, Roosevelt questioned the legitimacy of 254 of Taft's slightly more than five hundred delegates. If seventy of these delegates had been reversed, Roosevelt would have had the power to block Taft's nomination and likely assure his own. Because Taft initially controlled the convention, he determined the membership of the committee that made the decisions. Not surprisingly, that committee favored him in most cases, reversing only nineteen of the delegates and leaving Taft in clear control. In response, Roosevelt cried foul, charging Taft with theft, betrayal of the party, and numerous other crimes. Although a number of issues are still debated among historians, a few things are certain: Some of the challenged delegates should have been Roosevelt's, and Taft's forces clearly engaged in some delegate fraud because the committee agreed with nineteen of Roosevelt's challenges. Roosevelt, however, also presented some clearly bogus delegate claims. Of his more than two hundred challenges, two-thirds were thrown out immediately. As historian Francis Broderick concludes, "164 of Roosevelt's challenges were transparent shams."[28] Finally, the arguments over right and wrong had no effect in the end, and raw political power succeeded because of the nature of the nomination system. Nominations by caucuses and then conventions depended upon political organization and party control, not popular appeal. This type of system was inherently undemocratic and led to manipulation and fraud. In the end, both Roosevelt's challenge and Taft's response reflect more on the antidemocratic nomination system and an emerging redefinition of democracy than on the morality of either man.

By the time the Republican convention opened Taft controlled the proceedings, and his delegates nominated him on the first ballot. Control came at a high cost, however: Almost three-quarters of Roosevelt's delegates left the convention and the Republican party at Roosevelt's direction. Taft and the conservatives controlled the party, but the fight with Roosevelt had shredded the party. Roosevelt, on the other hand, now seized the moral high ground. Claiming to be the victim of the basest political fraud, Roosevelt took up the battle for democracy and clean politics. In leaving the convention he linked religion, morality, and politics by exclaiming, "We stand at Armageddon and we battle for the lord." This was a theme he would continue in August when he and his followers met again in Chicago, but for a new purpose: to hold the first convention of the Progressive party, and to nominate Theodore Roosevelt for president.

"Standing at Armageddon": Roosevelt and the Progressive Party

Although Roosevelt and his followers walked out of the Republican party, they quickly found it considerably more difficult to climb out of the Republicans' shadow; throughout the campaign Roosevelt's opponents labeled the new party as simply an extension of the Republican party.* In many ways these critics were right. Roosevelt was the most easily identifiable Republican; most of the leaders of Roosevelt's party were former Republicans; and the new party held its convention in Chicago, where just over a month earlier Roosevelt had fought for the nomination of the Republican party. However, the members of the convention that Roosevelt and his followers held in August 1912 looked nothing like the staid and austere people who had chosen Taft.

Taking the name of the progressive reform movement itself, the Progressive party was an emotional festival that was equal parts a call for revolution, Protestant revival meeting, forum for the inclusion of women in party politics, and hardheaded political convention that attempted to claim the symbols of political reform and radicalism as their own. Progressive reformers had gained emotional and moral power from the social gospel movement, which saw Christianity as a social system and politics as an expression of religious morality. Reflecting this trend, Roosevelt's followers sang hymns and revival songs throughout the con-

---

*See, for example, Document 22, Louis Brandeis's "Trusts, Efficiency, and the New Party."

vention, and Roosevelt entitled his acceptance speech "A Confession of Faith." (See Document 7.) Evangelical groups such as the Massachusetts delegation, which had prayed on the way to the convention and took as their purpose "translating the principles of Christianity into modern life," could not have been disappointed by the results.[29] In a fascinating move, the new party connected this religious message with revolutionary symbolism. Progressive party members, viewing themselves as a new force in American politics, adopted socialism's red handkerchief as their own symbol. Convention delegates were treated to the fascinating sight of Roosevelt using a red bandanna to lead the crowd in singing "Onward Christian Soldiers."

Red, however, wasn't the only symbolic color flying in Chicago. Throughout the convention yellow handkerchiefs and banners of the women's suffrage movement called attention to the increasingly important role women played in reform politics, despite their exclusion from voting. The Progressives provided a greater forum for female politicians than either major party. Jane Addams, who had founded and operated Chicago's famous settlement house, Hull House,* and who represented women's issues in reform ideology, was one of the important female delegates to the convention; she became the first woman to second the nomination of a presidential candidate when she spoke in support of Roosevelt. The major strains of progressive reform, Protestant moralism, radicalism, and the domestication of politics all came together on the Progressive stage in August, 1912.

An Almost Certain Victory: The Democratic Convention

As the Democratic party met in Baltimore in late June, political cartoonist John McCutcheon captured the situation facing the Democrats. McCutcheon's cartoon, "The Time, the Place, and the Girl," showed a female figure labeled "Opportunity" knocking at the door of the Democrats' house, ready to present a victory wreath and a banner reading "Victory for Some Real Progressive." Inside the house, Democratic leaders, distracted by fighting with each other, don't notice their visitor,

---

*Hull House, which opened in 1889, was America's best-known settlement house. Settlement houses were established by idealistic reformers (often women) who were looking both for an outlet for their talents and a way to solve the problems of urbanization, industrialization, and immigration. These reformers lived in working-class, immigrant districts and provided child care, job counseling, language classes, and many other necessary social services while at the same time attempting to influence the behavior of the people they were serving.

who sighs, "If someone doesn't come soon, I'll go to the next door" (where the Progressives reside). (See Document 29.) With three well-known candidates in the race, the Democratic convention was drawn out and difficult; although at one point it appeared that they might suffer from the same kind of internal squabbling that had divided the Republicans, the Democrats ultimately came together and chose the man who had been the initial front-runner for the nomination, New Jersey's Woodrow Wilson.

Wilson was in many ways the ideal candidate for the Democrats in 1912. Since their last presidential victory in 1892 the Democrats had lost three times with William Jennings Bryan's populism and once with the stolid conservatism of Judge Alton B. Parker.* Wilson could unite the party on any number of issues. Southern born, but a resident of a northern state, Wilson could appeal to the party's ex-Confederate core, while also drawing votes in urban and midwestern areas. Wilson also presented an image of rectitude, honor, and knowledge without appearing overly conservative; the son of a minister, he spoke in moralistic language that appealed to many reformers. Furthermore, Wilson's background struck a middle ground. In his academic writings he tended toward conservatism, but in his two years as governor of New Jersey, Wilson had taken on the language of the progressive reformers. He both applauded the economic reforms of La Follette and the other progressives in Wisconsin and came out for ballot reform, a lower tariff, and governmental regulation of big business to restore the power of the individual.[30] Finally, as a scholar of politics and history, Wilson seemed qualified to take over the presidency in an increasingly complex world, and as an academic he appeared to be above the political fray.

The same qualities that made Wilson the leading candidate, however, also placed him at a potential disadvantage. Although born in the South, he now lived in the North and finished second in most of the southern democratic primaries to Alabama's Oscar Underwood.† Simi-

---

*Bryan was a relatively unknown member of Congress from Nebraska in 1896 when he caught the attention of the Democratic National Convention with his "Cross of Gold" speech and won the Democratic presidential nomination at age thirty-six. Bryan lost the 1896 election to William McKinley, and ran again (unsuccessfully) in 1900 and 1908. In 1904 the Democrats nominated Alton B. Parker, a conservative judge from New York, whom Roosevelt defeated handily.

†As the majority leader of the House of Representatives (the second most powerful position in the House of Representatives), Underwood was a well-known Democrat who appeared more trustworthy to conservative southerners than Wilson, who had lived in the North and was embracing progressive reform.

larly, Wilson's recent conversion to progressive reform left many of Bryan's supporters unconvinced of Wilson's progressive credentials. Because Bryan had been the Democratic presidential nominee three times he was the single most influential person within the party, and it would be very difficult for anyone to gain the nomination without his support. Wilson tried to live down his 1907 statement that he hoped someone would "knock Mr. Bryan once and for all into a cocked hat," but throughout the primary season, he trailed behind Speaker of the House Champ Clark, who was from Bryan's neighboring state of Missouri and who had steadfastly supported Bryan before 1912.[31]

Consequently, Wilson came into the convention in Baltimore in July 1912 seriously weakened, and his condition seemed close to terminal as Clark took an early lead in the balloting. In fact, if the Democrats had followed the same rules as the Republicans (giving the nomination to the man with a majority of delegates), Clark would have been the Democratic nominee, and most likely the president. However, the Democrats required a two-thirds majority, which allowed Wilson to erode Clark's support and gain southern delegates opposed to Clark; finally, with Bryan's tepid support, Wilson became the Democratic nominee, four days after the first ballot had been cast. In any other election, Wilson's chances might have been destroyed by the party struggle, but in 1912, with Taft and Roosevelt already in the race, if Wilson could maintain his credentials as a progressive and hold on to Bryan's support, he would likely become president.

Socialism at High Tide: Eugene V. Debs and the Socialist Party

While most of the attention in the spring and fall of 1912 focused on the major parties and Roosevelt's new Progressive party, the field was further crowded by America's rising socialist movement. In 1910 and 1911 Socialist candidates had won mayoral elections in Schenectady, New York, and Milwaukee, Wisconsin, as well as lesser offices in a number of other cities and towns. By 1912 the Socialist party had over 100,000 members.[32] Furthermore, in *Appeal to Reason* the Socialists had a widely circulated weekly newspaper that both trumpeted the socialists' victories and mocked mainstream candidates, labeling Theodore Roosevelt, for example, as "Toothadore Busymouth—the would-be dictator and pawn of the capitalists."[33] Finally, in Eugene V. Debs the Socialists had the one candidate who could match Roosevelt in energy and enthusiasm, and a politician who could ensure that their views would get a true hearing. Debs had twice before run as the Socialist party nominee, in 1904 and 1908. Traveling across the nation in the 1908 race in the "Red Special" train, Debs had spoken six days a week and gained attention for his earnestness and relentlessness.

Debs was also able to make socialism less threatening to the traditionally antiradical American people. A native of the Midwest (born and raised in Terre Haute, Indiana), Debs subscribed to many of the religious and cultural ideals of his fellow citizens, and as Arthur Schlesinger Jr. notes, he had a "profoundly intuitive understanding of the American people. Men and women loved Debs even when they hated his doctrine."[34] Although the other candidates considered the Socialists important enough to challenge their doctrine, neither Roosevelt, Taft, nor Wilson engaged in overt red-baiting or demonization of Debs and his followers.[35] Debs's entry into the race assured that the American people would hear a radical message in 1912, and that most of them would at least listen when they did.

Debs's inclusion in the race did not mean that the Socialists were any more unified than their opponents. Although stronger in 1912 than at any previous time, the Socialist party was already showing signs of division. For years party members had debated whether Socialists should use violence to fight capitalism, but by 1912 this was no longer a theoretical debate. Under the direction of politically minded Socialists, the convention passed an amendment calling for the expulsion of any party member who used or advocated the use of violence in the struggles of the working class.[36] Although this maintained the party's electoral viability, it cut the party off from the most aggressive and energetic activists. Similarly, the nomination of a controversial campaign manager, J. Mahlon Barnes, split the party further. Barnes had been the party's national secretary until 1911, when party leaders dismissed him following an embarrassing sexual scandal. Barnes's selection for such a prominent post angered Debs, who denounced it as "a mistake and injustice," alienated Christian socialists, who saw radical economic doctrine as an extension of religious gospel, and reopened the moderate–radical debates in the party. Although Barnes stayed on throughout the campaign, in their infighting the Socialists mirrored the major parties and lost the chance to take advantage of the chaos in the Republican and Democratic ranks.

NOTES

[1]Eugene V. Debs, "A Year Supreme with Possibilities," *Appeal to Reason,* 867 (June 13, 1912): 4.

[2]John Milton Cooper Jr., *The Warrior and the Priest: Woodrow Wilson and Theodore Roosevelt* (Cambridge, Mass.: Harvard University Press, 1983), 156; William Howard Taft, "Address of President Taft at Youngstown, Ohio," May 14, 1912, *William Howard Taft Papers* (microfilm) series 9A, reel 570.

[3]Walter Lord, *A Night to Remember* (New York: Holt, Rinehart, and Winston, 1955), 100; Steven Biel, *Down with the Old Canoe: A Cultural History of the* Titanic *Disaster* (New York: W. W. Norton & Co., 1996), 25.

[4]Cooper, *Warrior and the Priest,* 141.

[5]In an interesting sign of how important the "progressive" designation was, the other candidates refused to concede it to Roosevelt. Wilson referred to Roosevelt and his followers as one wing of the Republicans. Both Taft and Louis Brandeis attempted to diminish Roosevelt's luster by labeling his followers the "New Party."

[6]William Howard Taft, speech at Elkton, Maryland, May 4, 1912, *William Howard Taft Papers* (microfilm), series 9A, reel 570.

[7]Debs, "Debs' Opening Speech of the Campaign," *Appeal to Reason,* 87 (Aug. 10, 1912): 1; Debs quoted in "Eugene V. Debs Says Moose Party Stole Socialist Planks," *Chicago Evening World,* August 15, 1912, found in *Papers of Eugene V. Debs* (microfilm), reel 7.

[8]Lewis L. Gould, "The Republicans Under Roosevelt and Taft," in *The Progressive Era,* ed. Lewis L. Gould (Syracuse: Syracuse University Press, 1974), 59.

[9]As quoted in Paolo Coletta, *The Presidency of William Howard Taft* (Lawrence: University Press of Kansas, 1973), 9.

[10]Robert M. La Follette, *La Follette's Autobiography: A Personal Narrative of Political Experiences* (Madison, Wis.: Robert M. La Follette Co., 1913), 331–37.

[11]Coletta, *Presidency of William Howard Taft,* 51.

[12]James Holt, *Congressional Insurgents and the Party System, 1909–1916* (Cambridge, Mass.: Harvard University Press, 1967), 25–26.

[13]As quoted in Coletta, *Presidency of William Howard Taft,* 50.

[14]Although the Congressional investigation ultimately cleared Ballinger of any wrongdoing, a minority report labeled him "an unfit man to hold the office of the Secretary of the Interior." As cited in Alpheus T. Mason, *Bureaucracy Convicts Itself: The Ballinger Pinchot Controversy of 1910* (New York: Viking Press, 1941), 179.

[15]Paul Wolman, *Most Favored Nation: The Republican Revisionists and U.S. Tariff Policy, 1897–1912* (Chapel Hill: University of North Carolina Press, 1992), 1–4.

[16]As quoted in Wolman, *Most Favored Nation,* 116.

[17]The 1908 Republican party platform pledged the party to "significant revision," but given the fact that Taft had spoken out for tariff reductions for more than a year and virtually all of the critics of the tariff wanted it reduced, it was logical to interpret the Republican platform as endorsing tariff reduction. George H. Mayer, *The Republican Party, 1854–1966* (New York: Oxford University Press, 1967), 303.

[18]As quoted in George E. Mowry, *The Era of Theodore Roosevelt* (New York: Harper & Row, 1958), 249; Wolman, *Most Favored Nation,* 152.

[19]Coletta, *Presidency of William Howard Taft,* 113–14; Holt, *Congressional Insurgents,* 36–37.

[20]"The National Progressive Republican League Declaration of Principals," 1–2, *La Follette Family Papers,* Manuscripts Division, Library of Congress, series B, box 138; Nancy Unger, *Fighting Bob La Follette: The Righteous Reformer* (Chapel Hill: University of North Carolina Press, 2000), 198.

[21] Roosevelt to Henry Cabot Lodge, April 11, 1910, *The Letters of Theodore Roosevelt,* vol. 7: *Days of Armageddon,* ed. Elting E. Morrison (Cambridge, Mass.: Harvard University Press, 1954), 71.

[22] Roosevelt to Sydney Brooks, October 17, 1910, *The Letters of Theodore Roosevelt,* vol. 7, 142–44.

[23] Roosevelt to Theodore Roosevelt Jr., August 22, 1911, *The Letters of Theodore Roosevelt,* vol. 7, 335–37.

[24] Roosevelt to Arthur Hamilton Lee, September 16, 1910, *The Letters of Theodore Roosevelt,* 129–31.

[25] Nancy Unger, "The 'Political Suicide' of Robert M. La Follette: Public Disaster, Private Catharsis," *The Psychohistory Review,* 21 (1993): 197–220.

[26] George E. Mowry, *Theodore Roosevelt and the Progressive Movement* (New York: Hill and Wang, 1946), 219.

[27] Roosevelt can be considered the master of his own demise. In 1908 Roosevelt's influence had helped kill a rule change that would have given more delegates to states that actually voted Republican and decreased the influence of Southern states. Mowry, *Theodore Roosevelt and the Progressive Movement,* 241; Richard Jensen, "Democracy, Republicanism and Efficiency: The Values of American Politics, 1885–1930," revised July 26, 2001, online at <http://www.vic.edu/~rjensen/rjensen/rj0025.htm> accessed July 8, 2002.

[28] Francis Broderick, *Progressivism at Risk: Electing a President in 1912* (New York: Greenwood Press, 1989), 54; Mowry, *Theodore Roosevelt and the Progressive Movement,* 237.

[29] *Chicago Tribune,* August 6, 1912, 5.

[30] Cooper, *Warrior and the Priest,* 27, 174.

[31] Ibid., 120.

[32] Tremendous Socialist Victories," *Appeal to Reason,* 833 (November 18, 1911), 1; Eugene V. Debs, *Writings and Speeches of Eugene V. Debs,* introduction by Arthur Schlesinger Jr. (New York: Hermitage Press, 1948), x.

[33] "Splendid Socialist Victory," *Appeal to Reason,* 772 (September 17, 1910), 1; "The Humor of It," *Appeal to Reason,* 773 (September 24, 1910), 4.

[34] Debs, *Writings and Speeches of Eugene V. Debs,* ix; Nick Salvatore, *Eugene V. Debs: Citizen and Socialist* (Urbana: University of Illinois Press, 1982), xii.

[35] This claim can be made for 1912; in earlier years Debs had been jailed for his labor activism, and during World War I, Wilson's Justice Department would prosecute Debs, under the Espionage Law, for his criticism of America's involvement in World War I.

[36] Salvatore, *Eugene V. Debs,* 255.

2

The Problem of the Progressive Era

Historians look for signposts in the past—evidence that stands out as remarkable or exceptional—and ask what made *this* time different? All of the energy, agitation, and conflict in 1912 serve as such a signpost, prompting questions such as: Why did such controversy break out in 1912? What was so unsettling for American politicians and the American people? The answer lies not just with the candidates or even politics, but in the basic economic, social, and political system in early twentieth-century America. Between 1877 and 1912, America's economic structure was in flux, and although there was little doubt that the United States would remain fundamentally capitalist, the form of that capitalism, and what kind of society it would shape, was constantly in question.

Although the debates ranged widely, there were two general camps: (1) Those who argued for a small-scale, localized, producer-oriented capitalism that favored individual manufacturers, shopkeepers, and proprietors—historians often refer to this as proprietary capitalism, and (2) Those who argued for a larger-scale capitalism based on massive, nationwide, organized businesses far too large to be run by an individual or group of partners—in short, the modern corporation. Historians refer to this as corporate capitalism.[1] Throughout the nineteenth century, the U.S. economy had favored individual proprietors, but a number of legal and technological changes now made it possible, if not necessary, to turn toward more organized, more efficient corporations. Although Roosevelt, Taft, Wilson, Debs, and others disagreed fundamentally on a number of issues, their debates focused on a central question: How should American society respond to the swift and sweeping social and political changes brought on by the development of this new corporate economy? Although this was inherently an economic question, its implications reached across American social and political life.

From Greenbackers to Populists: The Response to Change

The increasing importance of large-scale corporations in the U.S. economy between the 1870s and 1910 upset preexisting social and political patterns and produced a series of strikes, political protests, and reform campaigns by farmers, laborers, and middle-class professionals. In the early 1870s, farmers and borrowers were so angry with the federal government's decision to retire paper money issued during the Civil War that they formed the Greenback-Labor party in an attempt to resist what they thought was bankers' and financiers' control of the government.* As more American laborers entered factories and as laborers' influence over the workplace eroded in the last thirty years of the nineteenth century, labor strikes also became a common feature of American life. In Pittsburgh, Chicago, and other booming industrial cities, government troops confronted strikers; amid a wave of strikes in 1877 Americans feared a general labor rebellion.[2] At the same time, middle-class reformers† attacked the power of urban political machines and tried to break the control of political parties and their managers.[3]

All of this agitation reached its climax with the rise of Populism.‡ In the 1880s, farmers in both the Midwest and South, fearful of losing their place in the increasingly organized economy, began to form political and economic organizations of their own that called for easier credit, government regulation or ownership of railroads, and direct democracy§ to offset the political power of the economically powerful.[4] Politically, these organizations reached their peak in Kansas in 1890 when five People's party candidates, or *Populists* as they

---

*The Greenback-Labor party was a short-lived attempt to connect farmers' concerns with those of organized labor. Its presidential candidate, James Weaver, won 3.4 percent of the vote in 1880, but the party had ceased to exist by the late 1880s.

†Although these reformers, derisively nicknamed "Goo-Goos" for their demand for "good government," succeeded in instituting civil service reform, their reluctance to deal with anyone outside the middle class limited their power, and ultimately they failed to change the political system that troubled them.

‡*Populism* was a grassroots political movement predominately supported by farmers in the South and the Midwest. Although Populists' grievances varied, Populists tried to maintain small-scale capitalism and rural culture and resisted the rise of market-oriented capitalism and urban, industrial culture.

§*Direct democracy* involved shifting political power from elected representatives to the voters themselves. With the *initiative* and *referendum,* a proposed law was placed on the ballot, and if a majority of voters approved of it, it became law. The *recall* allowed voters to remove a public servant from office before his or her term was complete. In the *direct primary,* voters chose party nominees by popular vote, rather than through delegates at the party's political convention.

called themselves, won election to the U.S. House of Representatives and the Populists won control of the state's lower legislative house.[5] Although James Weaver, the Populist presidential candidate, received more than one million popular votes (out of more than 11 million votes cast) and twenty-two electoral votes in 1892, the Populists' national presence was short-lived. In 1896, the Democratic party nominated William Jennings Bryan, whose advocacy of monetary inflation co-opted the Populists' larger demand for debt relief and economic assistance for farmers, and by the turn of the twentieth century the Populists' grievances remained but the party was no longer an important factor in national politics.*

Although late-nineteenth-century protestors came from disparate backgrounds, behind their many complaints lay a central problem: The rising corporate economy, and the interdependent and organized society it created, left farmers and industrial workers feeling economically and socially powerless. Farmers felt the economic changes most acutely; despite the fact that they farmed more land and produced more crops per acre than they ever had, their collective share of the nation's income dropped by almost one-third between 1870 and 1890. As one rural historian concludes, "late-nineteenth-century farmers were increasingly vulnerable to forces beyond their control."[6] Industrial workers faced a different, and at times more confusing, economic and social challenge. On the whole, laborers' wages rose between 1870 and 1890, but as more and more people became employees, they lost control of their economic destinies. When industrial depressions hit in the 1870s and 1890s and unemployment rose to between 15 and 20 percent of the population, laborers felt their dependence and powerlessness most acutely.[7]

The Progressive Response

Americans responded to this rising sense of powerlessness and disaffection with a mania for reform. Collectively known as *Progressives* for their general belief in the ability of human society to progress toward

---

*Bryan's rousing speech advocating unlimited use of silver as a basis for American currency to aid debt-ridden farmers helped him secure the Democratic nomination in 1896. But after the Democrats nominated Bryan, the Populists were left with the choice of offering their own nominee, thereby splitting the votes for debt relief, or endorsing Bryan, and thereby making themselves subordinate to the more powerful Democrats. The Populists chose ideology over political organization and selected Bryan as their 1896 presidential nominee, leaving them politically irrelevant.

better conditions, reformers scrutinized key social, cultural, and political institutions, offering myriad solutions to the problems they identified. College-educated, native-born reformers moved into the center of urban immigrant life and opened up settlement houses to aid immigrants and industrial laborers. Although Chicago's Hull House has received the most attention, settlement houses flourished in most American cities, providing day care, job training, legal aid, English-language instruction, and a variety of other services. Christian ministers offered their own view of reform. Walter Rauschenbusch, for example, offered a new social gospel that connected religious morality with urban conditions.*

Although progressive reform began on the local level, in the late 1890s and early 1900s the demand for reform percolated up to state governments, and finally became a national concern during the presidency of Theodore Roosevelt.† The national mania for reform continued to grow even after Roosevelt left office in 1909, and by 1912 reached across social, economic, and geographic divisions. Consequently, unlike previous elections that had focused superficially and temporarily on the changes involved in the new economy, the political economic question of how to deal with the rising corporate economy, or *trusts,*‡ remained at the center of the debate between 1910 and 1912. This gave the country a chance to consider a wide variety of solutions to the problem. These solutions ranged from programs calling for the government to coordinate and manage corporate development to aggressive plans to roll back corporate development, to an indigenous American Socialist program that advocated common ownership of large-scale industries.

The Problem of Corporate Capitalism

But why did an issue that was fundamentally economic produce a series of *political* reforms and a climactic national election? The answer lies largely in the connection of economics to politics in the United States at

---

*Believers in the social gospel attempted to reform American society to live up to Christian virtues. Rauschenbusch was a Baptist minister who worked with immigrants in New York City. He provided the clearest description of the social gospel in his book *Christianity and the Social Crisis.*

†Roosevelt was president from William McKinley's death in 1901 until 1909.

‡Progressive Era politicians and reformers used the word *trust* loosely to mean any large-scale business organization that dominated an industry. In the early days of the new economy, American business leaders informally agreed on prices and access to markets to avoid ruinous competition. These informal agreements, however, could not be enforced, and they gave way to more structured corporations and combinations of corporations.

the turn of the twentieth century. American politicians had often invoked laissez-faire ideals, arguing that the government should not be involved in the economy; however, by the early twentieth century this was manifestly impossible.[8] In the mid-nineteenth century, changes in state laws had made it possible for the new corporations to develop. Because these corporations operated across state lines, they were outside the influence of local communities, leaving only the federal government with the reach and power to influence or control them. When Congress passed the Interstate Commerce Act in 1887 and the Sherman Antitrust Act in 1890, it acknowledged that the federal government had a central role in shaping and restraining economic concentration.[9]

Recognizing this role did not mean that the federal government had the means to control corporate growth and consolidation. In the years between 1897 and 1903 financiers created almost three hundred new interstate corporations, and by 1904 these corporate combinations controlled nearly 40 percent of manufacturing capital in the country.[10] Such a concentration of industrial power was unprecedented in the United States and many Americans, regardless of their political affiliation, worried that corporations might accumulate so much power that they would threaten key American values including democracy, individualism, and self-determination. Different strains of Progressivism attempted to address these widespread changes; the election of 1912 was important because the future shape of the country's economic and social system as well as the leadership and future of the progressive reform movement were at stake.

Although the candidates in the 1912 election had different views on how to address the problem, they agreed that concentration of wealth and corporate organization was the major challenge facing America during this period. Also, most political observers saw corporate power as a sign of a fundamental breakdown of American democracy. They believed that the new corporate giants could acquire so much economic power that they would corrupt the political process and become more powerful than the government itself. This fear is evident in Wilson's depiction of corporate power as an octopus-like menace: "the tentacles of these things [corporations] spread in every direction, and until we have broken their inside control, the government is helpless to assist the people." (See Document 24.) Roosevelt expressed the same idea more moderately when he spoke of the need to "prevent the political domination of money," and "to make our political representatives more quickly and sensitively responsive to the people whose servants they are." (See Document 1.) The debates over the rise and shape of the new economy were charged because the corporate question was at the heart of every issue—economic, social, or political—that came up in 1912. The corporate question was *the* question of the Progressive Era.

Although the question of corporate power came to a head in 1912, the roots of this issue reached back to the mid-nineteenth century. Although the U.S. economy grew from the 1820s onward, both the total production and the structure of industry changed rapidly and significantly between 1880 and 1912. Increased investment, technological advancement, and new forms of management allowed U.S. manufacturers to develop much larger, more complicated, and more productive enterprises than had ever existed. In the simplest terms, Americans produced more than one-third more per person between 1870 and 1900 than they had in the twenty years before the Civil War.[11] Two concepts—economies of scale and scope—were central to this growth.* By using large factories to their fullest capacity and by producing constantly, the new large enterprises reduced the cost of each individual item they produced. At the same time, they developed organizations to ensure that they would have an adequate supply of raw materials and the ability to sell the large quantity of finished goods they produced. In short, these new enterprises produced goods more *efficiently,*† making more for less.[12]

Organized Efficiency: The Modern Corporation

Central to this efficiency was a new form of organization: the modern corporation. Creating factories and businesses that could produce on a huge scale required both massive investment and centralized management that could regulate raw material supply, factory production, and efficient marketing. Corporations‡ separated management from ownership by creating a legal entity that was the product of investment capital. The corporation was controlled by a board of directors who

---

Scale refers to buying and producing in large quantities to reduce costs. *Scope* is "reach," or the ability to find markets for massive quantities of efficiently produced goods.

†Efficiency does not refer to how quickly something is produced but instead is a measure of the cost per unit. If one form of manufacturing can produce the same number of products at a cheaper cost per product than another form of manufacturing, it is economically more *efficient.*

‡Changes in the laws were also important in this process. In 1889 New Jersey changed its laws to allow one corporation to own stock in another, paving the way for corporate combinations, or mergers.

were not legally responsible for corporate behavior but were financially responsible to corporate investors. This allowed a variety of disconnected investors to pool their money, and it allowed corporations to conduct business nationally but with effective centralized control. For example, in the late nineteenth century, Andrew Carnegie* dominated steel production, investing huge sums of money into new technology and then plowing profits back into increasingly efficient plants. When investment banker J. P. Morgan† put together a powerful syndicate of investors, however, drawing together more than one hundred steel corporations with more than a billion dollars in capital, Carnegie sold his company to the newly created United States Steel Corporation.[13]

In the trend toward centralized management and increased efficiency, the new corporate giants often consolidated a number of individual enterprises. Because massive manufacturers produced goods more cheaply, they often took over markets from individually operated, proprietary businesses. In response, smaller businesses either sold out to their larger competitors or consolidated into larger, interstate operations that tried to retain control of markets and raw materials. In the 1880s, a southern businessman named James Duke mechanized cigarette production, only to produce many more cigarettes than he could sell. His overstock spurred him to create an extensive marketing organization and to consolidate with the other significant cigarette manufacturers into the American Tobacco Company. By 1900, the American Tobacco Company, or the tobacco trust as it was commonly known, produced at least half of the tobacco Americans purchased.[14] In short, new corporate enterprises leaned toward consolidation in order to stabilize prices, and smaller enterprises consolidated to defend themselves.

Whether an offensive or defensive strategy, consolidation was the order of the day at the turn of the twentieth century, and by 1910 many industries had come under the control of just one or two producers. Between 1895 and 1904, 319 new corporate combinations were formed. In this process, thousands of smaller, independent firms ceased to exist. At the end of the merger wave, at least fifty major industries were dominated by a single firm that controlled 60 percent or more of the output in that industry.[15]

---

*Carnegie was an immigrant from Scotland who had worked his way up to great wealth and was an excellent example of the American success story.

†Morgan was in many ways Carnegie's opposite. He organized groups of investors rather than spending his own capital, and established America's greatest investment bank, J. P. Morgan and Co., rather than building a factory or other industrial plant.

Two Responses to Corporate Growth

Americans were divided over the meaning of these changes. Some, like public-interest lawyer Louis D. Brandeis, feared the new corporations would destroy America's economic and social system and decried the "curse of bigness," whereas others, like Charles Van Hise,* author of *Concentration and Control,* viewed the rise of the massive and efficient new enterprises as a natural and inevitable evolution in American capitalism. Consequently, by the end of the nineteenth century, reformers were beginning to argue that the new corporations were the most pressing social and economic issue confronting American society.

Faced with increasing pressure to control corporate power, Congress passed the Sherman Antitrust Act in 1890. The law declared illegal "every contract, combination in the form of trust or otherwise," and stated that anyone "who shall monopolize . . . any part of trade . . . shall be deemed guilty of a misdemeanor." The Sherman Act seemed to make trusts and monopolies illegal, but by giving the federal government the power to control organized wealth, in the end the law created more confusion than it solved. First, Congress did not create a special body to enforce the antitrust law, but simply turned the decision to prosecute cases over to the attorney general. This linked economic decisions to politics, and guaranteed that trusts and economic organization would only become a greater focus of public attention. Second, because the Sherman Act left the courts to rule on the cases prosecuted by the attorney general, the precise meaning and application of the law was ambiguous. It wasn't entirely clear whom the law would be used against; although anticorporate activists hoped it would be used against the new corporations, its provisions could be used to attack labor unions as illegal "restraints of trade." Furthermore, the courts had difficulty defining and applying the Sherman Act. Between 1897 and 1911, the Supreme Court applied a stringent standard, ruling that all restraints of trade were illegal. In 1911, however, after a change in personnel, the Court reversed itself and applied a more lenient "rule of reason" that stated only that "unreasonable" restraints of trade were illegal.[16]

The tobacco and Standard Oil cases, in which the Court first established the new standard, provide illustrations of the confusion created

---

*Brandeis was an attorney from Massachusetts who was later appointed to the Supreme Court by Woodrow Wilson. Van Hise was president of the University of Wisconsin.

by the Sherman Act. On the surface, the Court seemed to rule against big business, by ordering both trusts to be broken up into a number of smaller units. By establishing the more lenient standard, however, which required the government to prove why a restraint of trade was "unreasonable" or against the public interest, the Court made the law less powerful. Furthermore, the Court's decision increased confusion over the government's role in controlling corporations and organized business and contributed to the stridency of the debates of 1912. Anticorporatists* like La Follette and Brandeis saw the decisions as proof that the Sherman Act needed strengthening.[17] Procorporate† figures like Van Hise, on the other hand, believed that the prosecutions showed the "impotency" of a legalistic approach.[18] Taft was stuck in the middle, justifying the prosecutions as stringent but not too stringent, a position that alienated both sides. In the end, the Sherman Act disappointed virtually everyone, its ambiguity simply making corporate power a more contentious issue than it had been previously. It failed to resolve the problem of corporate power in large part because the issue was simply too complex for any single law.

A "Machine for Making Money": The Corporation and American Society

The new, large-scale business organizations not only revolutionized economic production, but they profoundly challenged America's social and cultural system as well. In the nineteenth century, Americans equated business success with personal merit and believed that those who profited from doing business in a community had both a claim to leadership and a social responsibility to that community. Consequently, many Americans implicitly connected their social structure to the economic system. However, the new, massive businesses made

---

*Anticorporate leaders attacked corporations on both economic and social grounds, arguing that they were inherently dangerous. In their view, corporate profits were not the product of increased efficiency, but of ruthless and illegal business practices. Furthermore, they believed that the growing corporate economy damaged small-scale producers such as independent business owners and farmers. Their goal was to freeze or roll back corporate development.

†The term procorporate suggests that these leaders saw the new business combinations and the economy they shaped as a logical and positive development in American life. Procorporate leaders were not beholden to businesspeople, nor did they favor subordinating government to business. Instead they hoped to limit the noneconomic power of corporations through government regulation while benefiting from the increase in productivity the corporations brought. Procorporate leaders did not so much favor corporations as the development of the corporate economy.

this connection difficult to maintain. Because of their tremendous efficiency, corporations often squeezed out smaller, owner-operated businesses. Furthermore, the headquarters of these new giant enterprises
were often in states far away from where the businesses operated,
leaving local communities disconnected from business leaders and the
businesses themselves. Rather than having a single owner-operator
responsible for the success and operation of the plant, ownership was
spread across the nameless and faceless stockholders, most of whom
owned a tiny percentage of the company; the new corporations had
boards of directors and many tiers of managers, none of whom actually owned the company. Corporations could not provide political or
social leadership to a political community as proprietary business leaders had; instead, the corporation was, as one reformer noted, a
"machine for making money... [that] reduced men to the insignifi-
cance of numerical figures."[19]

In many ways the emerging corporate economy changed American
social life as much as it changed the economy. It affected not only
how people would work and invest but the fundamental bases of social
and political organization. Throughout the nineteenth century, American manufacturing moved from small handicraft shops to larger,
mechanized factories, affecting industrialization, urbanization, and
immigration. The rise in corporate production concentrated labor and
required more workers. This spurred the growth of metropolitan
American cities, as urbanization increased dramatically. Meanwhile
large numbers of immigrants came to American cities to work in factories or to provide services for those who did. In short, the growth of
the corporate economy was at the heart of America's emergence as a
modern, interdependent, and cohesive nation. Adjusting to this new
economy was the central challenge Americans faced in pursuit of
"progress."

By the end of the nineteenth century these changes had extended
into American politics, affecting the way both women and men viewed
themselves and their political representatives. In responding to these
changes women's suffrage* advocates developed a new, more flexible
argument that reinvigorated the demand for suffrage. As early as the
1890s, advocates of women's suffrage had argued that women should
have the vote not only because it was a right (the traditional argument

---

*Although women had been able to vote in New Jersey from 1776 to 1807, the formal
women's suffrage movement began in 1848 with the first Women's Right's Convention in
Seneca Falls, New York, which included the demand for the "sacred right" to vote.

that had driven suffrage) but also because in an increasingly urban, interdependent society, voting was the only way for women to fulfill their traditional obligations to home and family. Suffrage advocates like Jane Addams and others argued that society had changed so radically that only giving women the vote would allow them to retain control over traditional domestic life, child rearing, moral education, food preparation, and other traditionally "feminine" aspects of society.[20] In Addams's words, politics was now as much "municipal housekeeping" as statecraft, and in such an age women were experts whose leadership and votes were required to maintain order and morality.[21] In the interdependent, corporate, urban world, suffrage was both a social good and a personal right.

Whereas suffrage advocates saw in corporate power a new argument for expanded democracy, many other politicians worried that the rapidly rising power of the corporations had permanently damaged American democracy. One of the leading Progressive Republicans, Robert La Follette, argued that the money and organization that corporations in his state could provide to the party allowed them to control the caucus meetings that determined whom the party nominated for major offices and ultimately who was elected. La Follette then connected this political influence to society by noting that the tax structure and laws of his state favored large corporations, especially the railroads, because most of the legislators were influenced by the railroads. Politicians were not the only people to note this connection. Muckraking journalists like Ida W. Tarbell and Lincoln Steffens* published popular exposés pointing to the connection between political corruption and corporate power.[22] Similarly, in 1906, David Graham Phillips published *Treason of the Senate,* which argued that the Senate was fundamentally corrupt and controlled by a corporate-oriented hierarchy.[23] By 1912, many Americans had come to believe that democracy was in crisis, and that America's political and economic system were all of one rotten piece.

To reformers only a return to true democracy could solve this problem. Wisconsin led the move toward direct primary elections, as La Follette argued that breaking corporate control of the nomination process would break corporate legislative control. In California, Oregon, and other states the move to direct democracy spread further.

---

*Tarbell and Steffens were both journalists for *McClure's Magazine,* which gained attention (and subscriptions) by publishing investigations of corruption in American political and economic life. In 1902 Tarbell published an exposé of Standard Oil and Steffens revealed corruption in cities across the United States. Muckraking was a derisive term based upon the journalists' focus on the problems in American life.

These states passed constitutional changes allowing the people to sidestep the legislature and make their own laws through popular initiatives and referenda. At the same time, the people increased their power over elected officials by instituting the recall, which allowed the voters to remove an officeholder in the middle of the term of office if a majority of voters disapproved of his actions. As direct democracy spread across the states, people began to clamor for a national extension of these changes. By 1912, direct democracy had spread to national politics. In May 1912 the Senate approved an amendment to the U.S. Constitution that allowed voters to select their senators by direct election.* Also in 1912, for the first time, many states held popular primary elections to select delegates to the national convention. At the same time a number of candidates called for a national primary election, and two candidates called for the extension of democratic power over the judiciary. Attempts to restore democracy always had the specific goal of changing the laws that influenced American economic and social life; by the 1912 election, extending and expanding democratic power had become a national issue. And in the end, the 1912 election, and in many ways the Progressive movement itself revolved around two related issues: (1) How should the United States adjust to the powerful new corporate enterprises that developed in the late nineteenth and early twentieth centuries? and (2) How could democracy be maintained in the wake of economic concentration so that reinvigorated democracy could restrain economic concentration?

---

*The Seventeenth Amendment was approved by Congress on May 13, 1912; it was ratified by the states and became part of the Constitution on April 8, 1913, just one month after Woodrow Wilson took office.

NOTES

[1] As historian Martin Sklar notes, "The period 1890–1916 in United States history . . . was both an age of reform and the age of the corporate reconstruction of American capitalism." Sklar, *Corporate Reconstruction of American Capitalism, 1890–1916: The Market, The Law, and Politics* (Cambridge, Mass.: Harvard University Press, 1988), 1.

[2] Philip S. Foner, *The Great Labor Uprising of 1877* (New York: Monad Press, 1977), 101; Melvyn Dubofsky, *The State and Labor in Modern America* (Chapel Hill: University of North Carolina Press, 1994), 8–11.

[3] Morton Keller, *Affairs of State: Public Life in Late Nineteenth Century America* (Cambridge, Mass.: Harvard University Press, 1977), 520–22; Mark Wahlgren Summers, *The Gilded Age, or The Hazard of New Functions* (Upper Saddle River, N.J.: Prentice Hall, 1997), 186–92.

[4]Steven Hahn, *The Roots of Southern Populism: Yeoman Farmers and the Transformation of the Georgia Upcountry, 1850–1890* (New York: Oxford University Press, 1983), 270–71.

[5]Gene Clanton, *Populism: The Humane Preference* (Boston: Twayne Publishers, 1991), 53.

[6]David B. Danbom, *Born in the Country: A History of Rural America* (Baltimore: Johns Hopkins University Press, 1995), 134; Worth Robert Miller, "Farmers and Third Party Politics," in *The Gilded Age: Essays on the Origins of Modern America,* ed. Charles W. Calhoun (Wilmington, Del.: Scholarly Resources, 1996), 236.

[7]Eric Arnesen, "Workers and the Labor Movement in the Late Nineteenth Century," in Calhoun, *The Gilded Age,* 42.

[8]Historians have long recognized that laissez faire was an unachieved ideal in the United States in the nineteenth century, and government played a key role in shaping the economy. However, this recognition does not discount the fact that turn-of-the-twentieth-century Americans believed laissez faire to be a fact, not an unreachable goal. Robert A. Lively, "The American System: A Review Article," *Business History Review,* 30 (1955): 81.

[9]Keller, *Affairs of State,* 427.

[10]Samuel Hays, *The Response to Industrialism, 1885–1914* (Chicago: University of Chicago Press, 1957), 50.

[11]W. Elliot Brownlee, *Dynamics of Ascent: A History of the American Economy* (New York: Alfred A. Knopf, 1974), 189.

[12]Alfred D. Chandler pioneered the historical understanding of these terms in *The Visible Hand: The Managerial Revolution in American Business* (Cambridge, Mass.: Harvard University Press, 1977); for a valuable glossing of these terms, see Thomas K. McCraw, "Rethinking the Trust Question," in *Regulation in Perspective: Historical Essays,* ed. Thomas K. McCraw (Boston: Graduate School of Business Administration, Harvard University, 1981), 6–19.

[13]Hays, *Response to Industrialism,* 50–52.

[14]Brownlee, *Dynamics of Ascent,* 200; Stuart Bruchey, *Enterprise: The Dynamic Economy of a Free People* (Cambridge, Mass.: Harvard University Press, 1990), 348.

[15]In 1899 alone, more than one thousand firms disappeared in consolidations, Bruchey, *Enterprise,* 341; Hays, *Response to Industrialism,* 50.

[16] Sklar, *Corporate Reconstruction,* 127–46.

[17]The bill that Brandeis referred Wilson to in Document 22 was written by La Follette and Brandeis in part in response to the Standard Oil and Tobacco decisions. Alpheus T. Mason, *Brandeis: A Free Man's Life* (New York: Viking Press, 1946), 353.

[18]Charles R. Van Hise, *Concentration and Control: A Solution to the Trust Problem in the United States* (New York: Macmillan, 1912), 192.

[19]Robert M. La Follette, "Address of 1897," *La Follette Family Papers,* B211.

[20]Alice Stone Blackwell, "Twelve Reasons Why Women Want the Vote," *Woman Suffrage Leaflet,* 6, no. 4 (July 1893).

[21]Jane Addams, "Utilization of Women in Municipal Government," in *Jane Addams: A Centennial Reader,* ed. Emily Cooper Johnson (New York: Macmillan, 1960), 114.

[22]Ellen F. Fitzpatrick, ed., *Muckraking: Three Landmark Articles* (Boston: Bedford Books of St. Martin's Press, 1994).

[23]Louis Filer, *Crusaders for American Liberalism: The Story of the Muckrakers* (New York: Collier Books, 1961), 236–38.

3

The Candidates Debate

During the first decade of the twentieth century, American politicians frequently debated how best to resolve the nation's turmoil, but in the two years leading up to the election of 1912 the American people took part in a national dialogue on the fundamental organization of their society.[1] Political candidates drew from intellectual leaders and public sentiment, and by the time the voters went to the polls in 1912, they had been educated about all aspects of the country's economic and political structures. The questions under discussion extended far beyond politics, to the basic structure of American society in the twentieth century.

The Procorporatists: Theodore Roosevelt and Charles Van Hise

Theodore Roosevelt stood at the center of the campaign. Not only did the struggle for the Republican nomination come down to a question of whether he would enter the race, but his proposal for a strong federal commission to control the new corporate enterprises was hotly debated. Roosevelt stood out in 1912 because he alone believed that the rise of the new large-scale business organizations was natural, inevitable, and if properly managed, beneficial for the American people as a whole. In 1910 he had returned to national attention by delivering a series of speeches across the western half of the country in which he outlined his program of "New Nationalism." Roosevelt believed that the rise of new industrial forms, which both produced efficiently and created a single integrated economy, was necessary for national development. Consequently, he viewed combinations of wealth as inevitable and logical signs of economic progress and national unity and strength. As he explained in his New Nationalism speech, "Combinations in industry are the result of an imperative economic law which cannot be repealed by political legislation" (Document 1). In other words, the changes facing the American people were in many ways outside the control of individuals and their government, and the United States should accept the development of a corporate capitalist economy.

The recognition and acceptance of this new corporate economy was Roosevelt's most significant contribution to the debate, and he continued to sound this theme. In accepting the Progressive party nomination, Roosevelt spoke of the natural "evolution" of the economy, and in his "Charter of Democracy" speech in March 1912, he not only claimed that corporate development had "come to stay," but he argued that these changes were also "desirable." As he stated, "It is for the advantage of all of us to have the United States become the leading nation in international trade, and we should not deprive this nation . . . of the instruments best adapted to secure such international commercial supremacy" (Document 4).

Roosevelt wasn't concerned about wealth in general or even the size of businesses, but about the "conditions which enable . . . men to accumulate power which it is not for the general welfare that they should hold" (Document 1). Roosevelt saw a need for balance in assessing corporate power. On the one hand he rejected the idea that big businesses were inherently and automatically dangerous, but at the same time, he recognized that they could easily harm the society they were expected to serve. He drew this distinction carefully, stating, "I do not believe in making mere size of and by itself criminal. The mere fact of size, however does unquestionably carry the potentiality of . . . grave wrongdoing" (Document 4). The distinction, Roosevelt believed, came down to the behavior of corporate leaders themselves. If they behaved responsibly, society benefited. All too often, however, concentration of economic resources led to concentrations of power and "antisocial" behavior by those in charge of large corporations.

Although this distinction can be found in Roosevelt's words, it is not there directly. Instead, historians and students of history can indirectly draw this from Roosevelt's discussions. Roosevelt's statement that "immoral practices" must be prevented, his belief that America must make sure that all who gained great fortunes did so in an "honorable fashion," and his call for the government to be on the watch for the "wicked" and "antisocial" tendencies of corporate leaders make clear his belief that corporations had the ability to damage society. Corporations held the promise of positive results, but they could just as easily give in to bad behavior that would damage society. Roosevelt's opponents saw this as a vague definition, and they mocked him for trying to divine the difference between "good" and "bad" trusts.

Roosevelt appealed to his audiences to see the real-world consequences of corporate misbehavior. He noted the "suffering and injustice" when workers were injured on the job and then left to fend for themselves due to lack of concern by their employer and lack of adequate worker's compensation insurance. Roosevelt made clear to his audiences that the issue went beyond economic theory as he appealed, "I wish I had the power to bring before you the man maimed or dead, the women and children left to struggle against bitter poverty because the bread-winner has gone" (Document 4). But for Roosevelt the issue extended beyond those directly damaged by corporate misbehavior. All of the speeches in this collection (Documents 1, 4, and 7) refer to the danger of destroying "equality of opportunity" in America. In this phrase, Roosevelt spoke to the traditional American belief that open competition in a free market would allow every individual to succeed and fail on his or her own merits. He believed that by 1910 the new large-scale organizations were developing a "sinister influence" that blocked the individual from the "fair chance to make of himself all that in him lies" (Document 1). The danger of corporate power threatened the fundamental social and economic institutions of market capitalism and the fluid social structure that many Americans, including Roosevelt, associated with it.

"MORE ACTIVE GOVERNMENTAL INTERFERENCE":
ROOSEVELT'S CORPORATE REGULATION

To remedy this potential danger, Roosevelt proposed controlling the corporations with a program of national registration, "regulation," and "supervision" (Document 4). He was not afraid of the massive conglomerate businesses because he believed that government oversight would limit most dangerous aggregations of big business power, but he believed that this "more active governmental interference with social and economic conditions" was necessary to take full advantage of corporate power and efficiency (Document 1).

Roosevelt substituted his new program of government regulation over corporations for the traditional federal laws, particularly the Sherman Antitrust Act. In his emphasis on efficiency and production, and his distinction between good and bad corporate behavior, he disagreed with the views of the traditional antitrust movement—that big businesses were dangerous and government should simply break up large accumulations of capital. Although he believed that antitrust laws could help the government control corporations, "to treat the antitrust law as an adequate, or as by itself a wise, measure of relief and betterment is a sign not of progress, but of Toryism* and reaction" (Document 7).

Roosevelt's argument drew from and influenced a rising school of thought that emphasized national power, efficiency, production, and prosperity over other goals. This is clear in Roosevelt's belief that "business has to prosper *before* anybody can get any benefit from it," and in the work of one of his procorporatist colleagues, Charles Van Hise, the president of the University of Wisconsin and a classmate and friend of La Follette's. In early 1912, Van Hise released his book on corporate policy, *Concentration and Control,* from which Roosevelt quoted liberally in his acceptance of the Progressive party presidential nomination. (See Document 7.) Van Hise's work reveals the potentially radical implications of the procorporate emphasis on efficiency and national production. Rather than worrying about the potential dangers of corporate power as Roosevelt did, Van Hise thought the government should provide the conditions necessary for full corporate growth and efficiency, believing that these were ends in themselves. As he wrote, "Under modern conditions, cooperation not competition should be the controlling word" (Document 12). Van Hise reversed traditional American economic assumptions,† arguing that competition limited production, and that the measuring stick was not social distribution but total national economic production. Like Roosevelt, Van Hise hoped to moderate the ill effects of the increasingly powerful businesses, but for both men economic efficiency and power was a central goal.

"TO FREE OUR GOVERNMENT FROM MONEY IN POLITICS":
ROOSEVELT AND DIRECT DEMOCRACY

Nonetheless, Roosevelt had a broader vision than Van Hise. Because he feared the political and human consequences of concentrated economic power, he combined aggressive democratic political reform

---

Tory was a nickname for English conservatives and the American loyalists who refused to support the American Revolution. By using this term Roosevelt suggested that his opponents were backward-looking. For the origins of Woodrow Wilson's program, see Document 20.

†Traditional American economic thinking stressed competition because of the belief that open farm land provided everyone the opportunity to succeed, and that if open economic competition existed everyone would have a relatively equal chance to succeed.

with his procorporate ideas. He believed that changes in the political process, including the initiative, referendum, recall, popular primary, and direct election of senators, could increase individual political power, effectively checking the potential power of the corporations without restricting their economic efficiency and advantages. In his speech to the Ohio constitutional convention Roosevelt spoke of the changes to the "machinery" of government he thought necessary to "free our Government from the control of money in politics" (Document 4). Students studying Progressivism are often confused about the purpose of political reform; they wonder why nominations from primaries are better than those from conventions, and what difference the popular election of senators made? As Roosevelt's example shows, direct democracy had a higher goal: better government, particularly legislation that shaped an economy that was both powerful and fair. As Roosevelt stated in his "Charter of Democracy," the various tools of direct democracy are "not . . . ends in themselves, but . . . weapons . . . which will make the representatives of the people more easily and certainly responsible to the people's will" (Document 4). Structural political and electoral reform was the key tool in the Progressives' array of tools, but it was just that—a tool—and never the end in and of itself.

To understand the fundamental social and economic motives behind political reform, it is important to note how Roosevelt's democratic ideas developed throughout the campaign. Although Roosevelt displayed a strong understanding of the economic importance of corporate power in his "New Nationalism" speech in 1910, his appreciation of direct democracy lagged behind. (See Document 1.) It wasn't until he came to view himself as a victim of undemocratic politics after the Republican National Convention that he developed a national program of direct democracy. In the primary campaign, Roosevelt was the most popular candidate, winning the majority of delegates chosen through the vote of the people. These delegates alone, however, did not control the party, and Roosevelt lost because Taft controlled the vast majority of delegates chosen through party meetings. In other words, he lost because the nomination was not determined on the basis of popular democracy. Drawing on this experience, Roosevelt endorsed an increasingly aggressive form of national democracy in his "Confession of Faith" to the Progressive party (Document 7). Using the Republican convention as an example of the corruption of politics, Roosevelt now demanded the "right of the people to rule," and outlined a detailed program of democratic reform for both state and national politics. In the "Charter of Democracy" Roosevelt had talked of direct democracy as an option that individual states could choose, but in the wake of the Republican convention he saw democratic reform as a national issue, and began calling for national presidential primaries, direct election of senators, full disclosure of campaign funding, and the extension of the initiative nationwide (Documents 4 and 7). Although he continued to call for each community to shape direct democracy to fit its own needs, in his acceptance speech Roosevelt offered a truly national vision of democratic progressive reform.

ABOUT FACE: ROOSEVELT AND WOMEN'S SUFFRAGE

Roosevelt's interest in democracy led him to reverse his view on the single biggest democratic reform of the early twentieth century: women's suffrage. In his two terms in office Roosevelt had opposed a federal amendment guaranteeing women the vote, and as late as 1911 he was by his own admission a "tepid" supporter of suffrage, writing, "Women do not really need the suffrage although I do not think they would do any harm with it" (Document 9). But as Roosevelt's affinity for direct democracy grew, so did his support of voting rights for women, and after accepting the Progressive party nomination he declared himself a "flat-footed" supporter of women's suffrage. Roosevelt's switch was both practical and intellectually consistent. It was clear that many women would support his campaign if he endorsed suffrage, and Roosevelt was also far too intelligent not to have seen a contradiction between calling for direct democracy and opposing the extension of voting rights to nearly half of the adult population.

But Roosevelt's support of women's suffrage was also connected to his economic program itself. Many of the social reforms that he considered crucial to his plan to control the "antisocial" tendencies of corporate power were of particular interest to women. Worker's compensation legislation concerned women directly. Widows were often left to raise their families in the wake of their husband's death on the job; and many of America's working women labored to support their families because of the uncompensated death of a spouse (Documents 1 and 7). Similarly nineteenth- and early-twentieth-century American culture emphasized the moral nature of women, which meant that women could use moral issues such as prostitution, drunkenness, and child labor to enter politics and act as experts. By 1912 female reformers had long been working on domestic-related social issues; women had written the pioneering legislation in some of these fields, and they were a natural and logical group of experts for Roosevelt to appeal to. Roosevelt inverted this line of reasoning in a letter to social reformer Florence Kelley* in which he wrote, "All that is necessary to make the most ferociously intense believer in woman suffrage . . . is to convince me that women will take an effective stand against sexual viciousness"† (Document 9). In actuality, Roosevelt had come to see the importance of "an effective stand" against prostitution long after Kelley had, and it was his interest in social reform that made him an appealing candidate for female reformers. Finally, because women now served as experts on political issues related to women, reformers like Kelley and Jane Addams played an increasingly important political role, especially in state and local matters.[2] Roosevelt recognized this new power, promising to incorporate women into the new party and writing to Addams, "It is idle now to argue whether women can play their part in politics, because in this convention we saw the accomplished fact" (Document 9).

The final point of Roosevelt's reinvigorated democracy was a demand for popular rather than judicial control over the final interpretation of the Constitution. This was one of the most provocative ideas of the entire Progressive Era, and it drew the greatest criticism of any of Roosevelt's ideas. (See Document 32.) Roosevelt was most directly concerned with state court decisions striking down worker's compensation‡ and the social justice legislation that broadened his political appeal. These kinds of programs were crucial to compensate for the "wicked" and "antisocial" tendencies of large-scale corporations. Without the government's ability to intervene directly on behalf of those left behind in the new economy (the people Roosevelt described as the "crushable elements" in society) and to forcefully control the behavior of the new economic giants, Roosevelt's program would sacrifice social justice for economic production (Document 7). As Roosevelt noted, "The only effective way in which to regulate the trusts is through the exercise of the collective power of our people as a whole" (Document 7). The ability of the courts to thwart this collective power fundamentally threatened Roosevelt's attempt to harness the power of

---

*It is important to note that Roosevelt's letter to Kelley describing the connection between suffrage and social reform antedates by two months the "Charter of Democracy" speech in which he first set out his democratic program.

†This term was a genteel synonym for prostitution.

‡Until the early twentieth century, American legal doctrine held employees practically responsible for their own on-the-job injuries. Beginning in 1911, a number of states began insurance programs to provide benefits for workers injured on the job regardless of responsibility for the injury.

the new corporations for a public good—Roosevelt's controlling idea in 1912.

The Anticorporatists: Robert La Follette, Louis Brandeis, and Woodrow Wilson

In contrast to the Roosevelt–Van Hise procorporate approach stood a body of anticorporate ideas advocated by La Follette, Louis Brandeis, and Wilson. La Follette and Brandeis were good friends before 1912 and frequently conferred over political-economic issues, but after La Follette lost the nomination to Taft, Brandeis began advising Wilson and asking his friends to support Wilson's candidacy. (See Documents 18, 19, and 20.)* All three of these anticorporatists worked from a fundamentally different assumption about corporate power than Roosevelt. La Follette's description of business combinations as the product of "a criminal conspiracy," as well as Brandeis's fear of the "menace inherent in private monopoly and overweening commercial power" (Document 20) both illustrate the basic proposition that large business organizations were inherently unnatural and socially destructive.[3]

La Follette, Brandeis, and Wilson all believed that an economy made up of many small, independent economic producers would lead to both the most efficient and most democratic social and economic system. Consequently, they pushed for the aggressive extension of antitrust legislation, believing that the Sherman Act could be perfected to both restrain the activities of existing corporations and keep new combinations from coming together. They wanted, in Brandeis's words, "to make that Sherman law a controlling force—to preserve competition where it now exists, and to restore competition where it has been suppressed" (Document 20).

Although La Follette, Brandeis, and Wilson collectively developed a comprehensive political, economic, and social program to deal with America's rising corporate problem, they also emphasized different elements of the program individually. La Follette understood the political power of corporations and their impact on social and economic life; Brandeis worried about economic culture and the size of business,

---

*La Follette supported Wilson in the general election and in the first months of his presidency. Although he stopped short of endorsing Wilson publicly, he made it clear that he intended to vote for Wilson, and he was one of two Republicans to cross party lines and vote for Wilson's most important early piece of legislation: the Tariff Act of 1913.

seeing large businesses as inherently dangerous to individual proprietors;* finally, Wilson was able to connect the specific economic
issues of corporate power with the day-to-day concerns of the American public and American ideals.

RESTORING REPRESENTATIVE GOVERNMENT: LA FOLLETTE'S
DIRECT DEMOCRACY

Of the politicians included in this volume, La Follette was the most
broadly concerned with the political consequences of corporate power,
fearing that corporations would soon dominate all aspects of society.
He argued that corporate power was inherently dangerous and could
flourish only in an undemocratic political system. He stated that corporations "abrogated, nullified, and abolished the *natural* laws of trade
and commerce," and believed that the corporations were products of
"fraudulent and fictitious capitalization."[4]

La Follette focused his attention on the connection between the
political influence and economic power of trusts. In his view, economic
and political power went side by side, and in his speeches he sketched
out a menacing corporate power that controlled American economic
and political life. He believed that because politicians had failed to control corporate growth, a small number of powerful leaders had been
able to destroy economic competition and then use their profits to
control political nominations and offices. In essence, although elections were still held, corporate and trust leaders, through the political
parties, controlled who would be elected. As La Follette argued, "we
have the form of representative government . . . but the soul, the life of
the representative [government] is fast being lost to the people of this
country" (Document 14).

La Follette was arguably the clearest and ablest advocate of electoral reform. In campaigning before America's first presidential primary, held in North Dakota in April 1912, he stated, "If the initiative,
referendum and recall are good for North Dakota . . . why are they not
good nationally?" (Document 13). La Follette believed that corporate
organization was against the interests of the majority of the people,
and that political reform could protect vital social and economic interests. He claimed that if "the official and the citizen should be brought
face to face so that the citizen may lay his hand on the public official . . . and point the way he should go," this change would produce a

---

*Private businesses may be owned by an individual or be a partnership, but control
of the company, or shares of ownership, cannot be transferred without the agreement of
all of the owners. Public corporations' stock is traded in an open market, and anyone
willing to pay the going price can purchase a share (or many shares) of the company.

fundamental change in legislation (Document 13). La Follette had built his career on electoral reform, and, like Roosevelt, he believed that popular political reforms could shift the balance of political power back to individuals. But unlike Roosevelt, he expected this shift in power to lead to a wholesale roll-back of corporate economic power. Pointing to two particularly unpopular new laws—the recent tariff change and a currency bill that many saw as aiding eastern corporate financiers at the expense of average citizens in the Midwest—La Follette asked, "If the people of the United States had the referendum . . . do you believe the people of the United States would have approved that iniquitous legislation?" (Document 13).[5]

Because La Follette believed that fixing the political system would automatically roll back corporate power, his national program to control corporate power was simple. La Follette focused on the Sherman Antitrust Act and its amendments. He claimed that if he had been president during the initial stages of the rise of the great corporations and trusts, he would have forced the attorney general and his assistants to "commit . . . to memory" the Sherman Act and then would have directed them to vigorously enforce the law.[6] This approach verged on oversimplification, but the simplicity works from the basic assumption of corporate illegitimacy that was the foundation of the anticorporate approach. Furthermore, antitrust prosecutions, like political reform, were not ends in themselves to La Follette, but another weapon in the attempt to create a more equitable society for "the individual, the farmer, [and] the worker."[7] Anticorporate politicians like La Follette attacked trusts not out of a general dislike, but out of a fear of the social, economic, and political consequences of corporate power.

RESISTING BIGNESS: BRANDEIS'S ECONOMIC VISION

The same fear of the social, economic, and political consequences of corporate power that motivated La Follette was reflected in Brandeis's belief "that no methods of regulation . . . can be devised to remove the menace inherent in private monopoly and overweening commercial power" (Document 20). However, Brandeis worried far more about the economic power of large-scale organizations than their political influence. He believed that large corporations became big by buying out other businesses, squeezing out those who would not sell, and seizing control of an entire industry—not by producing efficiently. Consequently, he argued that the main economic problem with trusts was not size or efficiency, but the elimination of competition. In *Trusts, Efficiency, and the New Party,* published in *Collier's Magazine* in September 1912, Brandeis pointed to U.S. Steel's takeover of Carnegie

Steel as part of an attempt to eliminate competition rather than the creation of a more productive enterprise (Document 22). Brandeis turned around Van Hise and Roosevelt's assumptions that corporations grew large through efficiency and argued that only through constant consolidation could large enterprises continue to control the economy. He wrote, "No conspicuous trust has been efficient enough to maintain long as against the independents . . . without continuing to buy up . . . its successful competitors" (Document 22).

Brandeis focused primarily on protecting small business owners.[8] He was concerned that the process of "combination" destroyed competing businesses, and he attempted to create an economy more favorable to small and individual business owners without explicit reference to the rest of society. Brandeis believed that monopoly could not be made "good," because the large corporations that dominated the economy squeezed out the individual, small-scale businesses that he considered the backbone of the economy and democracy (Document 20). Consequently, Brandeis hoped to amend the antitrust laws to make it easier for "individuals who have suffered from illegal acts [at the hands of corporations] to secure adequate compensation" (Document 20).

In many ways all of the candidates in the election agreed that efficiency was the central issue in structuring the economy, but they disagreed on how to define and produce an efficient economy. Brandeis drew sharp distinctions between the anticorporate and the procorporate assumptions and solutions, arguing that only open competition could produce efficiency. Although his program relied on similar "machinery" to Roosevelt's and Van Hise's, Brandeis noted that slight differences in "details" could produce fundamentally different results (Document 20). He favored severely restricting, if not eliminating, corporate organization, and he believed that an economy that included a number of competitors forcing each other to improve, economize, and innovate would produce the best social and economic results.

Because Brandeis saw efficiency as a product of competition among small units, and because he believed that only unlawful consolidations produced large-scale monopolies, he drew sharp distinctions between his ideas and Roosevelt's. Brandeis opposed Roosevelt's program as a plan to "substitute monopoly for competition," and called the difference between the two programs "as fundamental as that between Democracy and Absolutism" (Documents 21 and 22). Brandeis's explanation that "The New Party [Roosevelt's Progressive party] declares that private monopoly in industry is not necessarily evil but may do evil," can be contested, but it is an acute analysis of

Roosevelt's position, and Brandeis's vehemence was based upon the fundamental political-economic disagreements between the two men (Document 20).

A QUICK STUDY: WILSON AND THE SOCIAL CONSEQUENCES OF CORPORATE POWER

Whereas Roosevelt, La Follette, and Brandeis all had a clearly defined position on corporate power long before 1912, Wilson came into the national campaign without a practiced understanding of the trust problem, or any easily definable plans for a solution. By the time Wilson began his speaking tour in September 1912, however, he was clearly under Brandeis's influence, and he provided a far greater social vision of anticorporatism than did either of his colleagues.

Wilson approached the issue of trusts and corporations from a social angle, concerned less with the economic system itself than with the society shaped by economic conditions. In his speeches he appealed to as broad an audience as possible and focused on general American ideals rather than specific programs. He captured the general tenor of the Progressive Era and the uncertainty of a society undergoing fundamental changes when he asked his audiences, "Are you satisfied that the gates of opportunity are just as wide open to the youngsters, to your sons, as they used to be? Do you think the channels for independent action in this country are as wide open as they used to be?"[9] Although he pointed to the same problems as La Follette and Brandeis, commenting that "the corporations are having a bigger voice in the government of this country than you are," Wilson connected the problems to long-held American cultural attachments to independence and social and economic opportunity. In the process, Wilson, the academic, converted his progressive campaign from one of economic theory to a defense of American heritage, tradition, and ideals.

Wilson also proved able to expand specific problems into broader social issues. In his Labor Day speech in 1912 (Document 23), he provided perhaps the most concrete example of the social danger posed by corporate and trust development. Whereas Brandeis focused on small business owners and operators, Wilson explained how the destruction of competition would affect the wages of all workers:

> If I am obliged to refrain from going into a particular industry by reason of the combination that already exists in it, I can't become an employer of labor, and I can't compete with these gentlemen for the employment of labor. And the whole business of the level of wages is artificially and arbitrarily determined. (Document 23)

Wilson showed workers how limiting the number of potential employers through corporate consolidation would lead to a similar limiting of laborers' options, and ultimately a drop in wages. In this broad illustration, Wilson explained in concrete terms why the economic problem of trusts and monopolies was a grave social problem affecting everyone. By relating the business-oriented problem of corporate and trust development to the more practical issue of jobs and wages, he expanded the social consequences of corporate development, uniting seemingly disconnected groups of laborers and working-class people with others harmed by corporate power (particularly Brandeis's small business owners).

Wilson's statements also help explain Progressivism's emphasis on social unity, the absence of class politics in America, and the almost universal rhetorical abhorrence of "special interest" legislation. Wilson opened his Labor Day speech by telling a working-class audience that he wanted to speak about workers' issues, "not because I regard the wage earners of this country as a special class, for they are not." Instead, Wilson expanded the definition of working men and women and the public by stating, "The wage earners of this country, in the broadest sense, constitute this country" (Document 23). He spoke to laborers not solely as laborers, but as a larger part of American society that was endangered by trusts and corporate power.

Although Wilson quickly translated the nation's economic problems into concrete social consequences, he was not able to clearly define solutions to these problems. Wilson never mastered the nuances of Brandeis's program; his statement, "I am for big business and I am against the trusts," missed Brandeis's fundamental belief that big businesses were by their nature socially destructive (Document 24). Understanding this weakness allows us to challenge Wilson's understanding of the problem and the solution and see the generality of Wilson's statement that under his administration trusts would be regulated, "by those processes, now perfectly discoverable, by which monopoly can be prevented and broken up" (Document 24). Wilson was clearly against corporate power, but he was unsure about how to restrain it.

Wilson was a relatively inexperienced politician and a representative of eastern Progressivism, which had emphasized social reform over the direct democracy that characterized midwestern Progressivism; therefore, he explored the relationship between political and economic reform somewhat reluctantly. In a speech at Sioux City he seemed to support the new direct democracy of the initiative, referendum, and recall, but he was clearly uncomfortable with these devices, noting that "I met a man who thought the referendum was some kind of animal because it had a Latin name" (Document 24). Similarly, Wilson stepped back from supporting the fullest extension of the recall and opposed the recall of judges. Finally, Wilson had long been against a federal amendment calling for women's suffrage, and he refused to change his position in 1912, despite what he thought was a flip-flop on the issue on Roosevelt's part. (See Documents 27 and 28.)* In the end, Wilson saw direct democracy as a threat, but one that he hoped would always be limited and one he feared himself.

The Best of a Bad Lot: African American Options in 1912

All four of the presidential candidates failed to include all Americans in their vision of democracy. For African American voters and leaders, the 1912 election offered no good choices. During his presidency, Theodore Roosevelt had shown limited but visible attention to the concerns of African Americans. In 1901 he hosted Booker T. Washington at a White House dinner, and he also nominated an African American lawyer to a federal judgeship. The Republicans never threatened Democratic dominance in the South, but the party of Lincoln (as the Republicans referred to themselves) provided the main avenue for African American political activity in the early twentieth century.

In 1912, however, Roosevelt cast African American voters aside. Taft had used his control of southern Republican delegations to defeat Roosevelt, and although the leaders of these delegations were white, African Americans made up the majority of southern Republican voters. In response to his defeat, Roosevelt resolved that the new Progressive party would accept disfranchisement of African Americans in the South. In organizing the new party in the South, Roosevelt's advisors followed a "lily-white" policy that effectively excluded African American delegates from the southern delegations of the new Progressive party. In a letter to one of his leading white, southern supporters, Roosevelt explained the new party's position. (See Document 10.) Although Roosevelt couched the exclusion of African Americans in paternalistic language, saying that the Progressive party would help southern African Americans by "appealing to the best white men" in the South, the meaning was clear: African Americans were not wanted in the party. In the end,

---

*Wilson changed his position on suffrage during World War I and called for voting rights for women as a wartime necessity.

the contrast between Roosevelt's support for an expansive democracy through women's suffrage and his rejection of democracy through the exclusion of black delegates appeared in physical form. Jane Addams, the first woman to second a presidential nomination, was immediately followed by a white, southern delegate who seconded Roosevelt's nomination by declaring, "I thank God there is a Dixie Land."[10]

Under Taft, the Republican party was no more welcoming to African Americans than the Progressives. In 1908 the Republicans had broken with tradition by not asking an African American party member to make a seconding speech for Taft. Furthermore, Taft supported a resolution that would have limited southern delegations to the proportion of the vote they provided nationally at each election and cut southern and African American delegations by more than two-thirds. The resolution failed to pass in 1908; ironically, if it had passed, the decrease in the size of the southern delegations that Taft controlled would have cost him the nomination in 1912. Once in office, Taft continued to ignore the political needs of African Americans. He did little to challenge white supremacy in the South, and in an age of segregation, disfranchisement, and racial violence, Taft's belief that "the greatest hope that the Negro has . . . in the south, is the friendship of and sympathy of the white men with whom he lives in the community," amounted to the abandonment of African Americans by the president and the Republican party.[11]

Faced with such limited options some African American leaders turned to an unlikely source: the Democratic party. In the years after the end of Reconstruction the "solid South" had consistently voted for the Democrats, who came to be seen as the protector of white supremacy. But faced with outright hostility and neglect from the Progressives and Republicans, some African American leaders, including W. E. B. Du Bois and Bishop Alexander Waters, overlooked the Democrats' connection to racism and endorsed Wilson.[12] Although born in the South, Wilson had lived for a long time in the North and had built his political career in New Jersey. Even as Wilson accepted the endorsement of white liberals and African American reformers, however, he showed an unwillingness to help African Americans by hiding behind federalism. In meeting with Oswald Garrison Villard (a grandson of one of America's most noted abolitionists and one of the founders of the NAACP) Wilson stated that although he opposed lynching, as president he would be unable to do anything about it because it was a state matter. Once in office, Wilson not only failed to help the cause of African Americans, he accepted his cabinet members' decision to segregate the federal bureaucracy. And in what must have been a particularly galling move, Wilson allowed D. W. Griffith's overtly racist *Birth of a Nation* to be shown at the White House.[13]

Even the Socialists proved of little assistance to African Americans in 1912. On the surface, the Socialists' belief in equality, their willingness to take radical and unpopular positions, and their experience with government suppression would suggest an openness to the challenges faced by African Americans. Most Socialists were also white, however, and they thought in racial as well as class terms. Victor Berger, one of the leading Socialist politicians, openly dismissed "negroes and mulattoes" as part of a "lower race."[14] Although Debs was more open-minded, he ultimately subordinated race to class. In 1903 he wrote that there was "no 'negro problem' apart from the general labor problem," and told potential African American supporters that the Socialist party had "nothing specific to offer the negro . . . the Socialist Party is the party of the working class, regardless of color—the whole working class of the whole world."[15] Debs believed that racial problems stemmed from economic structures and argued that socialism would bring social and racial equality. Although such an analysis may have been consistent with his political-economic convictions, it offered little more to African Americans than did the positions of Roosevelt, Taft, or Wilson.

Neither a "Flubdub" nor Second Rate: William Howard Taft

William Howard Taft has received less attention than other Progressive Era politicians and especially those involved in the election of 1912. Roosevelt's characterization of Taft as a "flubdub with a streak of the second rate" has stuck, and historians typically see him as a blunderer whose mistakes and inactivity split the Republican party in 1912. Those works that mention Taft in detail usually focus on his personal feud with Roosevelt and the fracture of the Republican party; this approach implicitly suggests that Taft had little to offer in the way of ideas or programs of his own in 1912.[16]

Taft was inherently legalistic and conservative. He was not a party politician by training or temperament, but a lawyer and judge. Consequently, he believed the challenges of the evolving corporate economy should be adjudicated according to existing law and precedent in order to maintain the social order, not as unsolved social issues that needed trailblazing legislative solutions. He did not see his role as providing creative or courageous leadership for Congress, the business community, or the American people; instead, he tried to follow as faithfully as possible the precedents he inherited. This was the outline of Taft's conservatism: a defense of existing institutions, a promise to follow the laws in place when he took office, and the belief that it was far safer to make the best of the machinery that already existed than to charge down unknown paths.

TAFT'S CONSERVATIVE VISION AND CORPORATE POWER

In practice, Taft neither lionized nor demonized corporations and economic concentration, but tried to maintain existing institutions and the social order. Like the procorporatists, he believed that size could produce efficiency, but he saw a cut-off point that distinguished him from Roosevelt and Van Hise. In his speech to the Academy of Political and Social Science, Taft stated, "It is true that the accumulation of plant will reduce the cost of production," but he noted that this was true only up to a point of diminishing returns, at which he believed that great size did not reduce costs for producers or consumers. (See Document 31.) Taft saw the possibility of greater efficiency with size, and he believed that if corporate organization could lead to greater national production it should be supported. Unlike Roosevelt—who saw the only danger in corporate and trust organization to be the antisocial acts of those who ran the corporation—Taft believed that there was an inherent problem in great size, and once a certain threshold had been passed, large-scale corporations were by their nature inefficient and antisocial. He commented that "when you enlarge the plant so that it covers the country, you increase the cost of production rather than reduce it; and the accumulation after that . . . is for the purpose of controlling the business and controlling prices" (Document 31). In essence, Taft started from the same goal of national production and maximum economic efficiency as Roosevelt, but drew different conclusions, which led him to significantly different actions.

The challenge for Taft was to find the proper dividing line between expansion for efficiency and expansion "not for the purpose of reducing the cost of production . . . but for the purpose of controlling the business and controlling prices" (Document 31). Taft used the Sherman Act, which Roosevelt had denigrated as his standard of measurement. Businesses produced by combinations that were guilty of "restraint of trade" had crossed over the threshold into "expansion for controlling prices," whereas those that could not be prosecuted under the Sherman Act fit Taft's definition of combinations that produced more efficiently. Undeniably this was a circular explanation that proved itself, and Taft suggested that combinations found guilty were by definition dangerous whereas those that were not prosecuted were beneficial to the community. However, this tautology reveals a great deal about Taft's understanding of the president's role in shaping the American economy.

In 1912 Taft noted that he enforced the Sherman Act because it "still remained on the statute book. It was there for enforcement under the oath which I had taken as President of the United States" (Document 31). Although he used the device of the anticorporatists—and used it far more than Roosevelt had during his two terms in office—Taft's application of the law and the results he achieved left the anticorporatists greatly disappointed with his leadership. When Taft noted his preference for negotiation and voluntary compliance by corporations with antitrust statutes rather than confrontation, he distinguished himself from the anticorporatists who saw large-scale corporations as something to be destroyed, not bargained with. Taft did not see the law as the means to create a social revolution; because he pursued antitrust prosecution only as legally necessary, his policies had very limited social and political influence and left the broader macroeconomic structure largely unchanged—precisely what the anticorporatists opposed.

"IT IS SAID I AM DISTRUSTING THE PEOPLE":
TAFT AND DIRECT DEMOCRACY

Because Taft saw corporate power as primarily an economic issue, and because he believed the problems of corporate concentration could be solved by using existing laws, he looked askance at the political innovations of the age. Taft did not fear corporate political dominance and saw little need for innovative direct democracy. He alone defended the existing political parties, and argued that they were crucial to the success of American democracy. He denigrated the new direct democratic machinery, focusing on the irrationality of majoritarian democracy and the need to protect private property. When he stated, "It is said I am distrusting the people [by rejecting direct democracy]," he tried to counter criticism of his own elitist statement that "the American people . . . have had the common sense . . . to face the fact that they can not trust themselves under all circumstances" (Document 30). Taft's political vision, however, was indeed elitist. Not only did he privately denigrate " the "ignorant and the lower class voter," but he publicly argued that the people were better off electing professional skilled legislators and accepting that not "everyone is fitted to do the professional work that may have to be done in behalf of the people" (Document 30). This stance was consistent with his legalism and his ideology, but it was politically costly in an age when people had come to believe that professional politicians became professionals by tying themselves to corporate-dominated political machines.

Behind Taft's defense of representative democracy lay a defense of constitutionalism and a direct attack on Roosevelt's evolving democratic reforms. Although Taft disagreed with the spirit behind turning legislation over to a direct vote of the people, he became truly animated after Roosevelt outlined his program for popular recall of legal decisions in his speech at Columbus, Ohio. In early March, Taft wrote, "The effect of Roosevelt's announcement [of his candidacy] and his Columbus speech has been sharply to call the attention of business men to the crisis that now impends" (Document 32). Taft feared that Roosevelt's challenge to the judiciary's supremacy in interpreting the Constitution would destroy important constitutional restrictions, including the Bill of Rights, and he believed that the importance of judicial supremacy superceded popular power.

Faced with this challenge, Taft presented himself as the defender of personal liberty, property rights, and the Constitution, and attacked Roosevelt as a demagogue and potential tyrant. (See Document 33.) Taft's goal was not victory in the national election, but winning the Republican nomination and control of the party, noting, "if I were nominated, even though I were to go down to defeat, I . . . should rally the conservative forces of this country and keep them in a nucleus of party strength" (Document 32). Taft believed that the recall of judicial decisions proposed by Roosevelt was truly radical because it not only threatened to produce bad laws, but would also undermine the Constitution itself. Taft argued that if a majority of the electorate could overturn judicial interpretation of the constitution, then the Bill of Rights itself could be negated. Speaking to an audience in New Hampshire, Taft envisioned a time in which popular passion would overturn the writ of habeas corpus and undermine the basis of personal liberty in the United States.*

---

*The writ of habeas corpus guarantees that anyone arrested by the government must either be charged with a specific crime or released by the government within a limited period of time. It protects individual liberty by limiting the government's police power. In his New Hampshire speech, Taft feared that constitutional rulings in favor of unpopular criminal defendants could be overturned by popular vote regardless of the merits of the case. In effect, this would make the protections of the Bill of Rights contingent upon popular approval.

Taft also outlined the particular danger Roosevelt's program posed for African Americans, pointing out that recall of judicial decisions could undermine constitutional guarantees produced by Reconstruction. In the years after Reconstruction African Americans had come to rely on the Fourteenth and Fifteenth Amendments to protect their civil and voting rights, and Taft suggested that a popular majority of white voters could simply reverse the application of these crucial amendments to the constitution.* Taft feared that Americans would follow a circular constitutional logic in which a law "must be constitutional because it is right, and whatever is right is constitutional" (Document 32). Although his positions were in many ways impolitic, as he himself recognized, they were not without merit. Taft challenged the "democratic" reforms of Roosevelt and La Follette and questioned the consequences and potential dangers of majoritarian rule, and it was this skepticism that explains his behavior throughout the election. Taft did have an unavoidable conflict with his opponents; however at its root the disagreement was over ideology, economics, and social policy, not personality.

Socialism as Progressivism: Eugene V. Debs and the Socialist Party

Socialism has rarely found fertile soil in American national politics, but in 1912, the concern over concentrated private economic power provided Eugene Debs and the American Socialist party with as favorable a position as they would find in the twentieth century. That the Socialists received their highest percentage of the national vote in 1912 (doubling the number of votes they had received four years earlier) was no fluke. The challenge of adapting to an integrated, corporate economy emphasized issues that fit well with socialist ideas. The self-regulating economic and social system promised by laissez-faire economics was already a thing of the past by 1912, making the economic control associated with socialism seem less intrusive and extreme. In a society increasingly defined by economic concentration, and in a period when politicians of all parties agreed that the federal government should play a significantly increased role in regulating the economy, the visible

---

*By 1912, the vast majority of African American voters in southern states had been disfranchised by changes in state laws and constitutions. Although the U.S. Supreme Court had not found this disfranchisement in violation of the Fourteenth and Fifteenth Amendments to the Constitution, these amendments remained the foundation of any hope for African American civil and political equality in the future.

hand of the government that socialism envisioned seemed less radical than in the past.

Furthermore, the basic socialist idea that production is a social process that no one can own, was the clearest understanding of the social and economic interdependence that was a central issue in Progressive Era development. The confluence of socialist and more mainstream ideas is found throughout the rhetoric of the campaign. Debs's statement that "society was divided into two classes—capitalists and workers, exploiters and producers" was common fare in Socialist discourse, and by 1912 it was not a far cry from more mainstream campaign rhetoric. Debs's assertion that "the capitalists, while comparatively few, owned the nation and controlled the government" (Document 39) seems identical to La Follette's claim that "A great power has grown up in the country, so great that men are asking whether it is stronger than the government" (Document 13).

Furthermore, in looking at the political economy of 1912, the Socialists and procorporatists emerge as odd intellectual cousins. Both groups saw the rise of corporate power as a logical and natural progression in American economics. In 1910, *Appeal to Reason* had argued, much as Van Hise had, that competition was a thing of the past and that "the trusts and monopolies of today are the natural development of industry." Debs's rejection of antitrust laws as "silly" and "puerile" followed Roosevelt's logic: If combinations were a necessary precondition for socialism, the attempt to break up these combinations was an attempt to reverse history. (See Document 38.) Debs commented that trying to return to precorporate conditions was the equivalent of "the protest of the stage coach against the locomotive and of the pony express against the railroad telegraph,"[17] drawing upon the same cultural image that Roosevelt did in denigrating the Sherman Act as a "flintlock" approach. Finally, Debs and the procorporatists agreed that the federal government should play a central role in managing the economy in order to keep economic oligarchs from developing (or in Debs's view, retaining) disproportionate political and social power. In short, some of the mainstream candidates and the Socialists saw a common political-economic problem of concentrated private power over industry and commerce—a shared vision that was as much a product of mainstream moves to the left to adapt to economic and social change as a Socialist move to the right.

"THE VITAL AND FUNDAMENTAL PRINCIPLES OF SOCIALISM"

Agreement on a problem, however, did not signal a common solution; and the Socialists forecast a future that stemmed from a different vision of social justice than did any of the other candidates in 1912. Debs dismissed the anticorporatists directly, arguing that they sought a past that could not be revived. Recognizing the similarity between Roosevelt's ideas and Socialism, Debs accused Roosevelt of stealing and perverting the Socialists' ideas, commenting, "The platform of the Roosevelt Progressive party has much in it with which the Socialists are in full agreement but it does not contain any of the vital and fundamental principles of Socialism" (Document 45).

Debs worked from a different, more expansive notion of democracy and equality than Roosevelt. He argued that corporations and trusts were a classic example of social production in which both a business and what it produced were greater than any of the individuals involved in them. Because trusts were a product of broad-based social relations, the only equitable and socially democratic solution was for the society as a whole to own such enterprises. As Debs asked, "shall the trust be privately owned by a relatively few and operated for their fabulous enrichment, or shall it be owned by the people in their collective, organized, and enlightened capacity and operated for the benefit of all?" (Document 37). From the same root problem of industrial concentration that animated the mainstream candidates, Debs drew a distinctly different conclusion that the problems of corporate capitalism were problems inherent in capitalism and could be solved only by a move away from capitalism itself.

"THE ECONOMIC AND POLITICAL UNITY OF THE WORKERS"

Debs's alternative understanding of economic and social equality shaped his views on political reform, as he came to see socialism as a necessary precondition for democracy. In his statement, "slowly but surely there is being established the economic and political unity and solidarity of the workers of the world," Debs provided a clear sequence and connection between labor organizing and political power. (See Document 40.) Consequently, Debs had relatively little use for direct democratic reforms or even political reform itself. Whereas the progressives viewed political reform as the means for social and economic reform, Debs expected social and economic power to produce political power. Union organization and working-class cohesion, not alterations in voting or legislation, were the means to power for Debs.

Furthermore, as opposed to the mainstream candidates, who saw the rise of large corporations as imperiling democracy, Debs saw them as a step toward socialist democracy. He described trusts as monuments to the "fact that competition has run its course . . . and that

cooperation has taken its place as the basis of a more perfectly organized society, a higher social order, and a more advanced civilization."
Debs saw democracy in social and economic equity rather than in
political participation (Document 37). Once workers developed their
power in the labor and economic arenas, they could consolidate it in
politics. Debs ignored the electoral reforms of the other candidates
not because he was apolitical, but because he saw justice and power
outside of party politics and intended to gain his power extrapolitically,
through industrial organization. In Debs's view, the rise of corporations made clear the choice between "industrial despotism and industrial democracy," a choice that made democracy and socialism all of
one piece. This was a complete reversal of the Progressive view of
political power as a tool to gain economic and social justice.

REFORM VERSUS RADICALISM

The Socialist documents included in this volume provide an important
contrast that reveals the basic economic assumption of Progressivism
and defines the terms of the arguments. The 1912 campaign revolved
around the question of who could best change and reform American
society. Capitalism itself, however, remained a central assumption.
Standing outside of capitalism, Debs recognized this limit in the
debate, and his statement that "the new Progressive Party is a party of
progressive capitalism . . . but it stands for the rule of capitalism all the
same," exposes the limits and cultural assumptions behind all of the
other candidates in the race (Document 39). The 1912 election was at
its heart a debate over how capitalism would operate, and although
there were many different types of capitalism considered, Debs recognized that the debate occurred within the limits of capitalist assumptions about property ownership, investment, and profit holding. Taft's
explicit defense of the unregulated right to private property may have
seemed conservative when compared with the views of Roosevelt, La
Follette, and Wilson, but in reality all agreed on the right to private
property and profits. This distinction refines the definition of Progressivism that emerged from the election of 1912.

Progressivism was at its heart a movement for reform of the existing structures of political, economic, and social life, and despite the
candidates' heated criticism of existing conditions, their movement
was a reaffirmation of traditional social and economic values, particularly capitalism. And, although Progressives did not intend to overthrow the system or break with past practice in American society, they
did understand that a more radical change would be possible if they

were not successful. At different times Roosevelt, La Follette, and Wilson were all branded as socialists, but Debs's example sharply distinguishes socialism from capitalist reform. The true radicalism of the American Socialist party in 1912 helps define the nature of progressive reform and draws a distinction between reform and radicalism.

Epilogue: The Debate Continued

Late in the evening of November 5, 1912, the Chicago sky lit up with a spotlight signal from the *Chicago Daily Tribune* announcing that the Democratic candidate, Woodrow Wilson, had been elected president. Although he had received only 42 percent of the popular vote, Wilson won a landslide victory in the electoral college, where he received 435 votes (or 82 percent). For a clearer statistical view of the election results, see Table 3.1. Roosevelt, with eighty-eight electoral votes and 27 percent of the popular vote, finished a distant second, and Taft became the only Republican in history to finish third with eight electoral votes and 23 percent of the popular vote.

Wilson's election was more than just a victory for the Democratic party (Democratic victory was a foregone conclusion after the Republicans split apart in Chicago). Wilson's election was an important transfer of leadership in political progressivism, and the election should ultimately be seen as an overwhelming ratification of progressive reform.

Although Wilson and Roosevelt had clashed throughout the fall, they had agreed on the same central challenge: reforming and adapting the political system to changing conditions. In speaking to his audiences Wilson presented a picture of a society in flux and outlined a view of the challenge America faced in adjusting to the rapidly evolving new economy. He stated, "The laws of this country have not kept

Table 3.1. *The 1912 Election: Final Results*

CANDIDATE	PARTY	POPULAR VOTE	PERCENTAGE OF POPULAR VOTE	ELECTORAL VOTE
Woodrow Wilson	Democrat	6,296,547	41.9	435
Theodore Roosevelt	Progressive	4,118,571	27.4	88
William Howard Taft	Republican	3,486,720	23.2	8
Eugene Debs	Socialist	900,672	6.0	0

up with the change of economic circumstances in this country; they have not kept up with the change of political circumstances in this country; and therefore we are not where we were when we started."[18] Roosevelt saw the same problem when he declared, "We are face to face with new conceptions of the relations of property to human welfare" (Document 1). Although they differed on the ultimate program, both men agreed on the need to adjust society to make economic "progress" produce more desirable political and social results.

Consequently, to understand fully the results of the election of 1912, Wilson's and Roosevelt's vote totals need to be seen together. Wilson and Roosevelt spoke for different reform programs, but they both spoke for reform; Taft alone could be said to be running on an explicitly conservative platform. When Roosevelt and Wilson's totals are combined, almost seven out of ten voters had favored a candidate running on an explicitly reformist platform. This figure is even higher (more than three out of four voters) when the remarkable support for Debs is included. By the time all the votes were counted, Debs had received more than nine hundred thousand votes (more than 6 percent of the popular vote), more than doubling his votes from the previous election and making the Socialist party as popular as it would ever be. Some of this rising vote is explained by the increasing popularity of Socialism on a local level, but a significant increase was likely due to the similarity between the Socialists' message and that of the more mainstream candidates.[19]

Furthermore, in the internal battle between the ultrareformist Roosevelt and Taft, the only openly conservative figure in the race, the results were more impressive. Roosevelt, running for a party that had not existed six months before the election against the Republican Taft, not only beat Taft in the popular vote (Roosevelt received 27.4 percent of the votes to Taft's 23.2 percent) but he humiliated Taft in the electoral college, gaining eighty-eight electoral votes to Taft's eight. Taft had denied Roosevelt the nomination and had succeeded in maintaining conservative control of the Republican Party. He could do nothing, however, to deny the popularity of Roosevelt or his reformist message, and Taft left the Republican party weaker than it had been at any time in its history.[20]

WOODROW WILSON AND THE ACCOMPLISHMENTS OF PROGRESSIVISM

Roosevelt and Wilson's support, however, continued even after the election. Wilson's first term in office marked the national high point of Progressivism as Congress, under Wilson's very public direction, passed a series of measures reforming the U.S. tax structure, banking system, antitrust laws, and corporate regulatory system. With the Democrats controlling both houses of Congress as well as the presidency, Wilson's success seems to reflect Democratic dominance and the success of the "New Freedom." On closer examination, however, Wilson's successes reflect the broader aims of Progressive reform, and not the single program of the "New Freedom."

Wilson's first task was to reform the federal tax structure. At his direction Congress quickly wrote a new tariff law to replace the divisive tariff that had doomed Taft's administration. In an important symbolic gesture, La Follette, the most prominent Republican Progressive in Congress, and Senator Miles Poindexter, a member of the Progressive party, supported the Democrats' new tariff law.[21] The new tariff reduced tax rates for consumers, and Congress further shifted the tax burden toward the wealthy when the Sixteenth Amendment became part of the Constitution in 1913. The creation of a federal income tax was the product of more than twenty years of agitation (the amendment had passed in Congress before Wilson took office), and Wilson deserves credit at most for helping to shape the first income tax laws. Regardless, with the new federal income tax and the new tariff law in place, the United States had what the reformers considered a "fairer" tax structure after 1913.

Whereas the institution of a federal income tax and the revision of the tariff was a common goal of almost all progressive reformers, restructuring America's archaic banking system required Wilson to mediate between two opposing reform philosophies. In one camp were reformers like Brandeis and William Jennings Bryan (whom Wilson had appointed as his secretary of state) who wanted the federal government to control the central bank in order to ensure access to capital for small business owners and farmers. In the other were advocates of private banking who believed that banking was an essentially private function that the federal government should help coordinate but not control or supervise. To complicate matters, these two camps split further on the issue of whether a new bank should be decentralized or controlled solely by a single institution. Wilson had few strong convictions on the issue, but he played a crucial role, helping to build political support for a compromise. The Federal Reserve system that emerged in December 1913 was a remarkable improvement over the private system that had existed before. It appealed to conservatives as well as a wide variety of reformers. The new system mirrored the U.S. federal system by establishing a single chairperson of the Federal

Reserve but delegating power to a dozen regional banks. Historian John Milton Cooper is correct in calling the Federal Reserve Wilson's "greatest single legislative monument," and it is a mark of the Federal Reserve's success, and the significance of Progressive reform, that the Federal Reserve Act of 1913 remains the fundamental banking law of the United States to this day.

The Democrats moved quickly on tariff and tax reform because there was a preexisting consensus for change. Although banking legislation had been more complicated and involved compromises, it too had been resolved in short time because of the clear need for reform. In dealing with the structure of the corporate economy itself, however, Wilson worked in pieces, ultimately combining ideas from the New Freedom and New Nationalism. In the fall of 1914, Wilson signed into law the Clayton Antitrust Act, a revision of the antitrust laws that defined "unfair" competition and made prosecutions easier to conduct. As originally written, the Clayton Act seemed to be the fulfillment of the New Freedom and Brandeis's plan to use antitrust laws to control corporations; however, the law that ultimately passed in Congress omitted their most important provisions.[22] Furthermore, at the same time that Congress passed the Clayton Act it passed a law, with Wilson's support, creating the Federal Trade Commission (FTC). Although Brandeis urged Wilson to support the creation of the FTC, it most clearly resembled the corporate regulatory commission that Roosevelt had called for in his "New Nationalism" speech in 1910. Wilson supported it in part to blunt Roosevelt's criticism before the upcoming congressional elections.

Having secured antitrust and corporate regulatory legislation, Wilson and Congress turned finally to social reform. In a series of small gestures Congress passed a worker's compensation law for federal employees, a law limiting railroad workers to eight hours of labor in one day, and a law outlawing child labor.[23] Although these laws applied to only a few hundred thousand workers at most, they were important symbolic gestures. In signing these bills into law, Wilson took the first steps in providing federal protection for the "crushable elements" of society that Roosevelt had spoken for.

On the surface, Wilson's blending of his own program with Roosevelt's ideas seems to suggest a reversal of his campaign rhetoric, but on deeper analysis, Wilson's first term in office reflected both the Progressive movement as a whole and the campaign of 1912. Progressivism wasn't the product of any single reformer's ideas and actions—instead it was a sustained, layered movement responding to the rise of a new, complex, corporate economy. Throughout the campaign reformers had debated ideas, developing them further in response to their opponents' programs. The progressive legislation that Wilson signed into law in his first term of office was the tangible extension of this debate. Wilson drew first and most importantly from his own program, but much as he had responded to Roosevelt during the campaign, in supporting the Federal Trade Commission and the later social legislation, Wilson adjusted his program to incorporate aspects of Roosevelt's plan. What emerged in the process was neither New Freedom nor New Nationalism, but Progressivism.

NOTES

[1] As John Milton Cooper notes, "For the only time except perhaps for Jefferson's first election in 1800, a presidential campaign aired questions that verged on political philosophy." Cooper, *Warrior and the Priest,* 141.

[2] Robyn Muncy, *Creating a Female Dominion in American Reform, 1890–1935* (New York: Oxford University Press, 1991), 26–27; Estelle B. Freedman, *Their Sisters' Keepers: Women's Prison Reform in America, 1830–1930* (Ann Arbor: University of Michigan Press, 1981), 57.

[3] La Follette, "An Open Letter to the Progressives of Nebraska," *La Follette Family Papers,* series B, box 215.

[4] La Follette speech at Bismarck, North Dakota, March 14, 1912, *La Follette Family Papers,* series B, box 215.

[5] La Follette speech at Jamestown, North Dakota, March 14, 1912, *La Follette Family Papers,* series B, box 215.

[6] La Follette, speech at Valley City, North Dakota, March 13, 1912, *La Follette Family Papers,* series B, box 215.

[7] La Follette, "An Open Letter to the Progressives of Nebraska."

[8] Thomas K. McCraw, "Rethinking the Trust Question," in *Regulation in Perspective,* ed. Thomas K. McCraw (Boston: Graduate School of Business Administration, Harvard University, 1981), 25–26.

[9] Woodrow Wilson, speech at Elk Point, South Dakota, September 17, 1912, in *The Papers of Woodrow Wilson,* vol. 25, ed. Arthur S. Link (Princeton, N.J.: Princeton University Press, 1978), 156–57.

[10] Paul D. Casdorph, *Republicans, Negroes, and Progressives in the South, 1912–1916* (University, Ala.: The University of Alabama Press, 1981), 148.

[11] Casdorph, *Republicans, Negroes, and Progressives,* 7.

[12] Cooper, *Warrior and the Priest,* 211.

[13] Although Wilson may not have been fully conscious of the racial content of the film, or the filmmaker's goal of blunting African American criticism of the film by getting the president's support, the fact remains that Griffith was able to quote from Wilson's *History of the American People* on the nobility of the Ku Klux Klan in the film. This quote, when combined with Wilson's tacit endorsement, provided inestimable aid for *Birth of a Nation* and grave disappointment to African American opponents of the film. Richard Schickel, *D. W. Griffith: An American Life* (New York: Simon & Schuster, 1984), 267–70.

[14] Nick Salvatore, *Eugene V. Debs, Citizen and Socialist* (Urbana, Ill.: University of Illinois Press, 1982), 226.

[15]Salvatore, *Eugene V. Debs,* 226.

[16]Taft, however, drew from both corporate and anticorporate ideas and adjusted these programs to produce distinctively conservative results.

[17]Debs, "Holds Socialism Gives Only Cure for Trust Evils," *Chicago Tribune,* November 25, 1912, found in *Papers of Eugene V. Debs* (microfilm), reel 7.

[18]Woodrow Wilson, "The Image of Progressivism," September 25, 1912, in *A Crossroads of Freedom: The 1912 Campaign Speeches of Woodrow Wilson,* ed. John Wells Davidson (New Haven: Yale University Press, 1956), 245–46.

[19]In 1910 Milwaukee had elected a Socialist mayor, Emil Seidel, and in 1914 a Socialist candidate received 21 percent of the gubernatorial vote in Oklahoma. John D. Buenker, *The History of Wisconsin,* vol. 4, *The Progressive Era,* ed. William Fletcher Thompson (Madison: State Historical Society of Wisconsin Press, 1998), 169; Salvatore, *Eugene V. Debs,* 234.

[20]Taft's electoral college vote decline, from 321 in his victorious campaign of 1908 to only eight in 1912, is by far the greatest in American political history. Herbert Hoover, the most unpopular incumbent president to receive his party's nomination, had a larger gross drop in electoral college votes (from 444 in 1928 to fifty-nine in 1932) but this was not nearly as great a decline when measured in percentage of original vote. Taft's electoral college vote in 1912 was only one-fortieth of his earlier vote, whereas Hoover's vote in 1932 was between one-seventh and one-eighth of his electoral college total in 1928.

[21]James Holt, *Congressional Insurgents and the Party System, 1909–1916* (Cambridge, Mass.: Harvard University Press, 1967), 89.

[22]Alan Dawley, *Struggles for Justice: Social Responsibility and the Liberal State* (Cambridge, Mass.: Belknap Press of the Harvard University Press, 1991), 148.

[23]The Supreme Court overturned the Keating-Owen Child Labor Act, just the kind of legalistic reversal of social justice that Roosevelt had protested against.

PART TWO

The Documents

4

The Procorporatists:
Theodore Roosevelt and Charles Van Hise

1

THEODORE ROOSEVELT

The New Nationalism
August 31, 1910

Soon after returning from Africa, Roosevelt embarked on a speaking tour in the western United States, the area in which he was most popular. The title of Roosevelt's political program came out of this speech, in which he spoke about creating a "New Nationalism"; however, the speech was most notable because it set down in specific terms Roosevelt's plan for how to deal with increasingly large, organized, and powerful businesses.

. . . In every wise struggle for human betterment one of the main objects, and often the only object, has been to achieve in large measure equality of opportunity. In the struggle for this great end, nations rise from barbarism to civilization, and through it people press forward from one stage of enlightenment to the next. One of the chief factors in progress is the destruction of special privilege. The essence of any struggle for healthy liberty has always been, and must always be, to take from some one man or class of men the right to enjoy power, or wealth, or position, or immunity, which has not been earned by service to his or their fellows. That is what you fought for in the Civil War, and that is what we strive for now.*

---

*Roosevelt delivered this speech to a group of Civil War veterans.

Theodore Roosevelt, *The Works of Theodore Roosevelt: National Edition*, vol. 27, ed. Hermann Hagedorn (New York: Charles Scribner's Sons, 1926), 5–22.

At many stages in the advance of humanity, this conflict between the men who possess more than they have earned and the men who have earned more than they possess is the central condition of progress. In our day it appears as the struggle of freemen to gain and hold the right of self-government as against the special interests, who twist the methods of free government into machinery for defeating the popular will. At every stage, and under all circumstances, the essence of the struggle is to equalize opportunity, destroy privilege, and give to the life and citizenship of every individual the highest possible value both to himself and to the commonwealth. . . .

Practical equality of opportunity for all citizens, when we achieve it, will have two great results. First, every man will have a fair chance to make of himself all that in him lies; to reach the highest point to which his capacities, unassisted by special privilege of his own and unhampered by the special privilege of others, can carry him, and to get for himself and his family substantially what he has earned. Second, equality of opportunity means that the commonwealth will get from every citizen the highest service of which he is capable. No man who carries the burden of the special privileges of another can give to the commonwealth that service to which it is fairly entitled. . . .

There can be no effective control of corporations while their political activity remains. To put an end to it will be neither a short nor an easy task, but it can be done.

We must have complete and effective publicity of corporate affairs, so that the people may know beyond peradventure whether the corporations obey the law and whether their management entitles them to the confidence of the public. It is necessary that laws should be passed to prohibit the use of corporate funds directly or indirectly for political purposes; it is still more necessary that such laws should be thoroughly enforced. Corporate expenditures for political purposes, and especially such expenditures by public-service corporations, have supplied one of the principal sources of corruption in our political affairs.

It has become entirely clear that we must have government supervision of the capitalization, not only of public-service corporations, including, particularly, railways, but of all corporations doing an interstate business. . . .

Combinations in industry are the result of an imperative economic law which cannot be repealed by political legislation. The effort at prohibiting all combination has substantially failed. The way out lies, not in attempting to prevent such combinations, but in completely controlling them in the interest of the public welfare. For that purpose the Federal

Bureau of Corporations is an agency of first importance. Its powers, and, therefore, its efficiency, as well as that of the Interstate Commerce Commission,* should be largely increased. We have a right to expect from the Bureau of Corporations and from the Interstate Commerce Commission a very high grade of public service. We should be as sure of the proper conduct of the interstate railways and the proper management of interstate business as we are now sure of the conduct and management of the national banks, and we should have as effective supervision in one case as in the other. The Hepburn Act, and the amendment to the act in the shape in which it finally passed Congress at the last session, represent a long step in advance, and we must go yet further. . . .

The absence of effective State, and, especially, national, restraint upon unfair money-getting has tended to create a small class of enormously wealthy and economically powerful men, whose chief object is to hold and increase their power. The prime need is to change the conditions which enable these men to accumulate power which it is not for the general welfare that they should hold or exercise. We grudge no man a fortune which represents his own power and sagacity, when exercised with entire regard to the welfare of his fellows. Again, comrades over there, take the lesson from your own experience. Not only did you not grudge, but you gloried in the promotion of the great generals who gained their promotion by leading the army to victory. So it is with us. We grudge no man a fortune in civil life if it is honorably obtained and well used. It is not even enough that it should have been gained without doing damage to the community. We should permit it to be gained only so long as the gaining represents benefit to the community. This, I know, implies a policy of a far more active governmental interference with social and economic conditions in this country than we have yet had, but I think we have got to face the fact that such an increase in governmental control is now necessary.

No man should receive a dollar unless that dollar has been fairly earned. Every dollar received should represent a dollar's worth of service rendered—not gambling in stocks, but service rendered. The really big fortune, the swollen fortune, by the mere fact of its size acquires qualities which differentiate it in kind as well as in degree from what is possessed by men of relatively small means. Therefore, I believe in a graduated income tax on big fortunes, and in another tax which is far more easily collected and far more effective—a graduated

---

* Created by Congress in 1887, the Interstate Commerce Commission oversaw railroad rates and was the federal government's first industrial regulatory body.

inheritance tax on big fortunes, properly safeguarded against evasion and increasing rapidly in amount with the size of the estate.* . . .

. . . We are face to face with new conceptions of the relations of property to human welfare, chiefly because certain advocates of the rights of property as against the rights of men have been pushing their claims too far. The man who wrongly holds that every human right is secondary to his profit must now give way to the advocate of human welfare, who rightly maintains that every man holds his property subject to the general right of the community to regulate its use to whatever degree the public welfare may require it.

But I think we may go still further. The right to regulate the use of wealth in the public interest is universally admitted. Let us admit also the right to regulate the terms and conditions of labor, which is the chief element of wealth, directly in the interest of the common good. The fundamental thing to do for every man is to give him a chance to reach a place in which he will make the greatest possible contribution to the public welfare. Understand what I say there. Give him a chance, not push him up if he will not be pushed. Help any man who stumbles; if he lies down, it is a poor job to try to carry him; but if he is a worthy man, try your best to see that he gets a chance to show the worth that is in him. No man can be a good citizen unless he has a wage more than sufficient to cover the bare cost of living, and hours of labor short enough so that after his day's work is done he will have time and energy to bear his share in the management of the community, to help in carrying the general load. We keep countless men from being good citizens by the conditions of life with which we surround them. We need comprehensive workmen's compensation acts, both State and national laws to regulate child labor and work for women, and, especially, we need in our common schools not merely education in book-learning, but also practical training for daily life and work. We need to enforce better sanitary conditions for our workers and to extend the use of safety appliances for our workers in industry and commerce, both within and between the States. Also, friends, in the interest of the working man himself we need to set our faces like flint against mob-violence just as against corporate greed; against violence and injustice and lawlessness by wage-workers just as much as against lawless cunning and greed and selfish arrogance of employers. If I could ask but one thing of my fellow countrymen, my request would be that, whenever they go in for reform, they remember the two sides,

---

*Because of restrictions in the Constitution, a federal income tax was not legal until the passage of the Sixteenth Amendment in 1913.

and that they always exact justice from one side as much as from the other. . . .

I do not ask for overcentralization; but I do ask that we work in a spirit of broad and far-reaching nationalism when we work for what concerns our people as a whole. We are all Americans. Our common interests are as broad as the continent. I speak to you here in Kansas exactly as I would speak in New York or Georgia, for the most vital problems are those which affect us all alike. The National Government belongs to the whole American people, and where the whole American people are interested, that interest can be guarded effectively only by the National Government. The betterment which we seek must be accomplished, I believe, mainly through the National Government.

The American people are right in demanding that New Nationalism, without which we cannot hope to deal with new problems. The New Nationalism puts the national need before sectional or personal advantage. It is impatient of the utter confusion that results from local legislatures attempting to treat national issues as local issues. It is still more impatient of the impotence which springs from overdivision of governmental powers, the impotence which makes it possible for local selfishness or for legal cunning, hired by wealthy special interests, to bring national activities to a deadlock. This New Nationalism regards the executive power as the steward of the public welfare. It demands of the judiciary that it shall be interested primarily in human welfare rather than in property, just as it demands that the representative body shall represent all the people rather than any one class or section of the people. . . .

. . . Of course, economic welfare is necessary, for a man must pull his own weight and be able to support his family. I know well that the reformers must not bring upon the people economic ruin, or the reforms themselves will go down in the ruin. But we must be ready to face temporary disaster, whether or not brought on by those who will war against us to the knife. Those who oppose all reform will do well to remember that ruin in its worst form is inevitable if our national life brings us nothing better than swollen fortunes for the few and the triumph in both politics and business of a sordid and selfish materialism.

If our political institutions were perfect, they would absolutely prevent the political domination of money in any part of our affairs. We need to make our political representatives more quickly and sensitively responsive to the people whose servants they are. More direct action by the people in their own affairs under proper safeguards is vitally necessary. The direct primary is a step in this direction, if it is associated with a corrupt-practices act effective to prevent the advantage of the man willing recklessly and unscrupulously to spend money over his more honest competitor. It is particularly important that all moneys received or expended for campaign purposes should be publicly accounted for, not only after election, but before election as well. Political action must be made simpler, easier, and freer from confusion for every citizen. I believe that the prompt removal of unfaithful or incompetent public servants should be made easy and sure in whatever way experience shall show to be most expedient in any given class of cases. . . .

2

DETROIT NEWS

Making a New Platform

September 10, 1910

MAKING A NEW PLATFORM.

This cartoon, which was drawn in the wake of Roosevelt's New Nationalism speech, played off of the themes that Roosevelt emphasized at Osawatomie, Kansas, and in other speeches on his western tour. "Trust regulation" is the centerpiece of the new platform, much as it would be the heart of the 1912 election.

Detroit News, September 10, 1910, 1.

3

THEODORE ROOSEVELT

Letters to Theodore Roosevelt Jr., Benjamin Barr Lindsey, and Chase Salmon Osborn
August 22, 1911, December 5, 1911, and January 18, 1912

In these letters Roosevelt considered the problems and promises of running for the Republican presidential nomination against William Howard Taft.

Theodore Roosevelt Jr. was Roosevelt's second child and oldest son and was almost twenty-four years old when he received his father's letter. Benjamin Lindsey was a judge and juvenile justice reformer in Denver, Colorado. Chase Osborn was governor of Michigan and a Roosevelt supporter. Along with seven other Republican governors, Osborn helped to generate the "demand" that Roosevelt run against Taft.

To Theodore Roosevelt, Junior

NEW YORK, AUGUST 22, 1911

Dearest Ted:

... I think Taft is considerably stronger than he was last November. The Insurgents have played into his hands because they have not been coherent, and they have tended to go to extremes. Gifford Pinchot is a dear, but he is a fanatic, with an element of hardness and narrowness in his temperament, and an extremist. La Follette has lost ground very much. There is no use in saying "I told you so," but if the Insurgents a year ago had followed my lead, they would have been infinitely better off....

Taft will be nominated, and as things are now I am not at all sure that La Follette will make a fight against him, although I think that having gone so far he would be foolish not to make the fight, simply as a point of honor. My present intention is to make a couple of speeches for Taft, but not to go actively into the campaign. Woodrow

Theodore Roosevelt, *Letters of Theodore Roosevelt,* vol. 7, ed. Elting E. Morrison (Cambridge, Mass.: Harvard University Press, 1954), 335–37, 450–52, 484–85.

Wilson still remains the strongest as Democratic Candidate, but he has lost and not gained during the last few months. There is a good chance of Harmon's being nominated. I hope we can carry Taft through, and there would be a fair chance against Harmon, although much less of a chance against Wilson. But I do not care for Taft, indeed I think less of him as time goes on, in spite of the fact that I believe he is improving his position before the people. He is a flubdub with a streak of the second-rate and the common in him, and he has not the slightest idea of what is necessary if this country is to make social and industrial progress. He does not even know what the problems are that confront our civilization, not to speak of realizing their seriousness. However, during my thirty years in politics, for nine tenths of the time I have been accustomed to make the best I could out of the second-best and the second-rate. I think Taft a better president than McKinley or Harrison, and I thoroughly distrust the Democratic Party.* But it is an awful pity that when Taft had such a chance as he had, and when the progressives were in control of the Republican Party and moving along the path of rational progress, he should have thrown over his chance and hurt the party and the country by so acting as to identify conservatism with reaction, and to deprive the progressives of leadership and permit them to run every which way to destruction.

Ever your father

To Benjamin Barr Lindsey

PRIVATE & CONFIDENTIAL

NEW YORK, DECEMBER 5, 1911

My dear Judge Lindsey:
... I very emphatically feel that to me personally to be nominated in 1912 would be a calamity. There is absolutely nothing for me to gain thereby. I dare say I should be defeated, for poor Taft, with the assistance of Aldrich, Cannon and others, has put a burden upon the Republican Party under which any man who attempts to lead it will stagger.† Moreover, there would be all kinds of well-meaning puzzle-headed people who, if I were nominated, would talk about a third

---

*Benjamin Harrison and William McKinley were the last two Republicans to serve as president before Roosevelt. Harrison won election to a single term in 1888, and McKinley was elected in 1896 and reelected in 1900 with Roosevelt as his running mate. When an assassin killed McKinley in 1901, Roosevelt became president.

†Senator Nelson Aldrich and Congress member Joseph Cannon were the two most powerful conservative Republicans in Congress in 1911.

term, entirely forgetting that the reason for the third-term theory can only concern itself with a third consecutive term, that is, with a man who is in office and has been in office for eight years, and is able to use on his own behalf the power of the Government; the reasoning cannot possibly apply to a man who is out of office. Moreover, some good silly people would vaguely feel that there had been an injustice to Taft, and even though they had complained bitterly about Taft while there was a chance of nominating him, they would, with the inconsistency of human nature, turn round and feel sorry for him if he were not nominated. . . . Suffice it to say that it seems to me that it would be from my standpoint a very great misfortune to be nominated, and that I am not yet convinced that the public need would be met by such nomination. I think the possibilities of slander and mendacity in misrepresenting me are so great, and the influences that would find expression in such slander and mendacity so powerful, that it would be a very doubtful experiment to try to nominate me or to try to elect me if nominated. Moreover I am absolutely certain that it would be criminal folly under any circumstances to nominate me unless it could be made clear as day that the nomination came not through intrigue or political work, not in the least to gratify any kind of wish or ambition on my part, but simply and solely because the bulk of the people wanted a given job done, and for their own sakes, and not mine, wanted me to do that job. I do not think that there will be any such demand, in fact I believe that the chances are infinitesimal that when the time comes there will be even any appearance of such a demand; but if ever the nomination should come I would not dream of even considering its acceptance unless it came in such a manner and on such grounds.

On the other hand, I have never felt that I was warranted in saying, what so many of the adherents of Mr. Taft, and, latterly, a few of the adherents of Mr. La Follette, and of course always the special representatives of privilege in all its forms, have urged me to say, namely, that I would not accept the nomination under any circumstances. Of course the special champions of Mr. Taft, and the special representatives of privilege and of special interest, are anxious above all things to get me to take some step which would remove what they regard as the threat of my return into public life. They are quite incapable of believing that I am sincere in saying that I do not want the nomination, and that I do not for one moment believe that it will be necessary for me to take it; and therefore they would be quite incapable of believing that I would be sincere if I should add what to you, speaking confidentially, I should add:—that of course circumstances might conceivably arise when I should feel that there was a duty to the people which I could not shirk, and so would accept the nomination. On no other terms would I ever dream of accepting it, and I do not, as I have said before, for one moment believe that these circumstances will arise, and that there will be any such real public demand for me and need for me as to make it my duty to accept. But you, my dear fellow, are entitled to have me speak candidly. Remember, however, that what I say is for your ear alone. I would not in the least mind your showing this letter or speaking of it to Jim Garfield (who naturally is for La Follette) or to my son-in-law Nick Longworth (who of course is for Taft) or even in the strictest confidence showing it to Governor Johnson of California, for whom I have a very high regard. But it must not be shown to anyone else, or spoken of to anyone else, for the average individual would be quite incapable of discriminating between what I have said to you and the mere bald statement that "Roosevelt would accept if nominated."* Do let me see you whenever you come anywhere near New York.

Very sincerely yours

To Chase Salmon Osborn†

NEW YORK, JANUARY 18, 1912

My dear Governor Osborn:

Events have been moving fast during the last few weeks. I am inclined to come to the conclusion that it is impossible for me much longer to remain silent. In this morning's mail came two letters from Governor Glasscock of West Virginia and Governor Hadley of Missouri, written to the same general effect as yours. I have written to each of them as follows:

"I have been thinking over matters a good deal the last few days, and even since I dictated this letter. It may be the best and wisest thing for me to come straight out and answer the questions you put to me in some public statement. Now if so, it seems to me very important it should be done in the right way. What do you think of having you and Governor Glasscock of West Virginia, Governor Stubbs of Kansas, Gov-

---

*James Garfield had served as Roosevelt's secretary of the interior and was a strong supporter of Roosevelt's conservation policy. Nicholas Longworth was Roosevelt's son-in-law and a member of Congress from Taft's home state of Ohio. Hiram Johnson was Governor of California and a well-known reformer. In 1912 he was named as Roosevelt's running mate on the Progressive party ticket.

†Chase Osborn was governor of Michigan and a noted Roosevelt supporter. For another view of Osborn, see Document 32.

ernor Osborn of Michigan, and Governor Bass of New Hampshire, write me a letter to which I could answer. I mention these Governors because I have received letters from them about the time I received yours. It seems to me that if such a group of four or five Governors wrote me a joint letter, or wrote me individual letters which I could respond to at the same time and in the same way, that such procedure would open the best way out of an uncomfortable situation. I am now inclined to think, as I did not even think as late as a month ago, that the evil of my speaking out publicly is less than the evil of my refraining from speaking. The letter to me might simply briefly state the writer's belief that the people of his State, or their States, desire to have me run for the Presidency, and to know whether in such a case I would refuse the nomination. I want to make it very clear that I am honestly desirous of considering the matter solely from the standpoint of the public interest, and not in the least from my own standpoint; that I am not seeking and shall not seek the nomination, but that of course if it is the sincere judgment of men having the right to know and express the wishes of the plain people that the people as a whole desire me, not for my sake, but for their sake, to undertake the job, I would feel in honor bound to do so."

What do you think of the plan? If you think well of it, would you mind writing to Governor Johnson of California on the subject? It seems to me that this offers the proper way to get at the situation.

Sincerely yours

4

THEODORE ROOSEVELT

A Charter of Democracy
February 12, 1912

This speech to the delegates of Ohio's constitutional convention was Roosevelt's first major address after announcing his decision to challenge Taft for the Republican nomination. In addition to restating his economic program, Roosevelt came out strongly for direct democracy, most

Theodore Roosevelt, *The Works of Theodore Roosevelt: National Edition,* vol. 17, ed. Hermann Hagedorn (New York: Charles Scribner's Sons, 1926), 119–48.

notably proposing that some state judicial decisions be subject to popular approval. His judicial plan drew the greatest negative attention of any of his ideas and convinced some Republicans that Roosevelt was a dangerous radical. (See Documents 32 and 33.)

... I believe in pure democracy. With Lincoln, I hold that "this country, with its institutions, belongs to the people who inhabit it. Whenever they shall grow weary of the existing government, they can exercise their constitutional right of amending it."

We Progressives believe that the people have the right, the power, and the duty to protect themselves and their own welfare; that human rights are supreme over all other rights; that wealth should be the servant, not the master, of the people.

We believe that unless representative government does absolutely represent the people it is not representative government at all.

We test the worth of all men and all measures by asking how they contribute to the welfare of the men, women, and children of whom this nation is composed.

We are engaged in one of the great battles of the age-long contest waged against privilege on behalf of the common welfare.

We hold it a prime duty of the people to free our government from the control of money in politics.

For this purpose we advocate, not as ends in themselves, but as weapons in the hands of the people, all governmental devices which will make the representatives of the people more easily and certainly responsible to the people's will....

I hold it to be the duty of every public servant, and of every man who in public or private life holds a position of leadership in thought or action, to endeavor honestly and fearlessly to guide his fellow countrymen to right decisions; but I emphatically dissent from the view that it is either wise or necessary to try to devise methods which under the Constitution will automatically prevent the people from deciding for themselves what governmental action they deem just and proper.

It is impossible to invent constitutional devices which will prevent the popular will from being effective for wrong without also preventing it from being effective for right.

The only safe course to follow in this great American democracy is to provide for making the popular judgment really effective....

We should discriminate between two purposes we have in view. The first is the effort to provide what are themselves the ends of good government; the second is the effort to provide proper machinery for the achievement of these ends.

The ends of good government in our democracy are to secure by genuine popular rule a high average of moral and material well-being among our citizens.

It has been well said that in the past we have paid attention only to the accumulation of prosperity, and that from henceforth we must pay equal attention to the proper distribution of prosperity. This is true. The only prosperity worth having is that which affects the mass of the people. We are bound to strive for the fair distribution of prosperity. But it behooves us to remember that there is no use in devising methods for the proper distribution of prosperity unless the prosperity is there to distribute. I hold it to be our duty to see that the wage-worker, the small producer, the ordinary consumer, shall get their fair share of the benefit of business prosperity. But it either is or ought to be evident to every one that business has to prosper before anybody can get any benefit from it. Therefore I hold that he is the real Progressive, that he is the genuine champion of the people, who endeavors to shape the policy alike of the nation and of the several States so as to encourage legitimate and honest business at the same time that he wars against all crookedness and injustice and unfairness and tyranny in the business world (for of course we can only get business put on a basis of permanent prosperity when the element of injustice is taken out of it). . . .

What is needed is, first, the recognition that modern business conditions have come to stay, in so far at least as these conditions mean that business must be done in larger units, and then the cool-headed and resolute determination to introduce an effective method of regulating big corporations so as to help legitimate business as an incident to thoroughly and completely safeguarding the interests of the people as a whole. . . .

It is imperative to exercise over big business a control and supervision which is unnecessary as regards small business. All business must be conducted under the law, and all business men, big or little, must act justly. But a wicked big interest is necessarily more dangerous to the community than a wicked little interest. "Big business" in the past has been responsible for much of the special privilege which must be unsparingly cut out of our national life. I do not believe in making mere size of and by itself criminal. The mere fact of size, however, does unquestionably carry the potentiality of such grave wrong-doing that there should be by law provision made for the strict supervision and regulation of these great industrial concerns doing an interstate business, much as we now regulate the transportation agencies which are engaged in interstate business. The antitrust law does good in so far as it can be invoked against combinations which really are monopolies or which restrict production or which artificially raise prices. But in so far as its workings are uncertain, or as it threatens corporations which have not been guilty of antisocial conduct, it does harm. Moreover, it cannot by itself accomplish more than a trifling part of the governmental regulation of big business which is needed. The nation and the States must cooperate in this matter. . . .

In other words, our demand is that big business give the people a square deal and that the people give a square deal to any man engaged in big business who honestly endeavors to do what is right and proper.

On the other hand, any corporation, big or little, which has gained its position by unfair methods and by interference with the rights of others, which has raised prices or limited output in improper fashion and been guilty of demoralizing and corrupt practices, should not only be broken up, but it should be made the business of some competent governmental body by constant supervision to see that it does not come together again, save under such strict control as to insure the community against all danger of a repetition of the bad conduct. The chief trouble with big business has arisen from the fact that big business has so often refused to abide by the principle of the square deal; the opposition which I personally have encountered from big business has in every case arisen, not because I did not give a square deal, but because I did.

All business into which the element of monopoly in any way or degree enters, and where it proves in practice impossible totally to eliminate this element of monopoly, should be carefully supervised, regulated, and controlled by governmental authority; and such control should be exercised by administrative, rather than by judicial, officers. No effort should be made to destroy a big corporation merely because it is big, merely because it has shown itself a peculiarly efficient business instrument. But we should not fear, if necessary, to bring the regulation of big corporations to the point of controlling conditions so that the wage-worker shall have a wage more than sufficient to cover the bare cost of living, and hours of labor not so excessive as to wreck his strength by the strain of unending toil and leave him unfit to do his duty as a good citizen in the community. . . .

So much for the ends of government; and I have, of course, merely sketched in outline what the ends should be. Now for the machinery by which these ends are to be achieved; and here again remember I only sketch in outline and do not for a moment pretend to work out in detail the methods of achieving your purposes. . . .

In the first place, I believe in the short ballot. You cannot get good service from the public servant if you cannot see him, and there is no more effective way of hiding him than by mixing him up with a multitude of others so that they are none of them important enough to catch the eye of the average, workaday citizen. The crook in public life is not ordinarily the man whom the people themselves elect directly to a highly important and responsible position. The type of boss who has made the name of politician odious rarely himself runs for high elective office; and if he does and is elected, the people have only themselves to blame. The professional politician and the professional lobbyist thrive most rankly under a system which provides a multitude of elective officers of such divided responsibility and of such obscurity that the public knows, and can know, but little as to their duties and the way they perform them. The people have nothing whatever to fear from giving any public servant power so long as they retain their own power to hold him accountable for his use of the power they have delegated to him. . . .

I believe in providing for direct nominations by the people, including therein direct preferential primaries for the election of delegates to the national nominating conventions. Not as a matter of theory, but as a matter of plain and proved experience, we find that the convention system, while it often records the popular will, is also often used by adroit politicians as a method of thwarting the popular will. . . .

I believe in the election of United States senators by direct vote. Just as actual experience convinced our people that Presidents should be elected (as they now are in practice, although not in theory) by direct vote of the people instead of by indirect vote through an untrammelled electoral college, so actual experience has convinced us that senators should be elected by direct vote of the people instead of indirectly through the various legislatures.

I believe in the initiative and the referendum, which should be used not to destroy representative government, but to correct it whenever it becomes misrepresentative. . . .

The power to invoke such direct action, both by initiative and by referendum, should be provided in such fashion as to prevent its being wantonly or too frequently used. I do not believe that it should be made the easy or ordinary way of taking action. In the great majority of cases it is far better that action on legislative matters should be taken by those specially delegated to perform the task; in other words, that the work should be done by the experts chosen to perform it. But where the men thus delegated fail to perform their duty, then it should be in the power of the people themselves to perform the duty. . . .

There remains the question of the recall of judges. . . .

I do not believe in adopting the recall save as a last resort, when it has become clearly evident that no other course will achieve the desired result.

But either the recall will have to be adopted or else it will have to be made much easier than it now is to get rid, not merely of a bad judge, but of a judge who, however virtuous, has grown so out of touch with social needs and facts that he is unfit longer to render good service on the bench.

It is nonsense to say that impeachment meets the difficulty. In actual practice we have found that impeachment does not work, that unfit judges stay on the bench in spite of it, and indeed because of the fact that impeachment is the only remedy that can be used against them. Where such is the actual fact it is idle to discuss the theory of the case. Impeachment as a remedy for the ills of which the people justly complain is a complete failure. A quicker, a more summary, remedy is needed; some remedy at least as summary and as drastic as that embodied in the Massachusetts constitution. And whenever it be found in actual practice that such remedy does not give the needed results, I would unhesitatingly adopt the recall.

But there is one kind of recall in which I very earnestly believe, and the immediate adoption of which I urge. . . .

When the supreme court of the State declares a given statute unconstitutional, because in conflict with the State or the National Constitution, its opinion should be subject to revision by the people themselves. Such an opinion ought always to be treated with great respect by the people, and unquestionably in the majority of cases would be accepted and followed by them. But actual experience has shown the vital need of the people reserving to themselves the right to pass upon such opinion. If any considerable number of the people feel that the decision is in defiance of justice, they should be given the right by petition to bring before the voters at some subsequent election, special or otherwise, as might be decided, and after the fullest opportunity for deliberation and debate, the question whether or not the judges' interpretation of the Constitution is to be sustained. If it is sustained, well and good. If not, then the popular verdict is to be accepted as final, the decision is to be treated as reversed, and the construction of the Constitution definitely decided—subject only to action by the Supreme Court of the United States. . . .

Now, the power to interpret is the power to establish; and if the people are not to be allowed finally to interpret the fundamental law, ours is not a popular government.

The true view is that legislators and judges alike are the servants of the people, who have been created by the people just as the people have created the Constitution; and they hold only such power as the people have for the time being delegated to them. If these two sets of public servants disagree as to the amounts of power respectively delegated to them by the people under the Constitution, and if the case is of sufficient importance, then, as a matter of course, it should be the right of the people themselves to decide between them. . . .

A typical case was the decision rendered but a few months ago by the court of appeals of my own State, the State of New York, declaring unconstitutional the Workmen's Compensation Act.* In their decision the judges admitted the wrong and the suffering caused by the practices against which the law was aimed. They admitted that other civilized nations had abolished these wrongs and practices. But they took the ground that the Constitution of the United States, instead of being an instrument to secure justice, had been ingeniously devised absolutely to prevent justice. They insisted that the clause in the Constitution which forbade the taking of property without due process of law forbade the effort which had been made in the law to distribute among all the partners in an enterprise the effects of the injuries to life or limb of a wage-worker. In other words, they insisted that the Constitution had permanently cursed our people with impotence to right wrong, and had perpetuated a cruel iniquity; for cruel iniquity is not too harsh a term to use in describing the law which, in the event of such an accident, binds the whole burden of crippling disaster on the shoulders least able to bear it—the shoulders of the crippled man himself, or of the dead man's helpless wife and children. . . .

I know of no popular vote by any State of the Union more flagrant in its defiance of right and justice, more short-sighted in its inability to face the changed needs of our civilization, than this decision by the highest court of the State of New York. Many of the judges of that court

---

*Throughout the nineteenth century and into the twentieth century, American legal doctrine generally held injured workers responsible for their own injuries. However, beginning in 1911, a number of states instituted worker's compensation insurance programs that paid workers who were injured on the job regardless of who was at fault for the injury.

I know personally, and for them I have a profound regard. Even for as flagrant a decision as this I would not vote for their recall; for I have no doubt the decision was rendered in accordance with their ideas of duty. But most emphatically I do wish that the people should have the right to recall the decision itself, and authoritatively to stamp with disapproval what cannot but seem to the ordinary plain citizen a monstrous misconstruction of the Constitution, a monstrous perversion of the Constitution into an instrument for the perpetuation of social and industrial wrong and for the oppression of the weak and helpless. . . .

Now, gentlemen, in closing and in thanking you for courtesy, let me add one word. Keep clearly in view what are the fundamental ends of government. Remember that methods are merely the machinery by which these ends are to be achieved. I hope that not only you and I but all our people may ever remember that while good laws are necessary, while it is necessary to have the right kind of governmental machinery, yet that the all-important matter is to have the right kind of man behind the law.

5

CHARLES McCARTHY AND THEODORE ROOSEVELT

Letters

October 21, 1911, and October 27, 1911

In this exchange of letters, Roosevelt and Charles McCarthy, a political reformer from Wisconsin and head of Wisconsin's legislative reference library, considered ways to curtail judicial power in order to give popularly elected political reformers more independence and power to shape laws.

Charles McCarthy and Theodore Roosevelt, letters, *La Follette Family Papers,* Manuscripts Division, Library of Congress, series B, box 68.

October 21, 1911.

Colonel Theodore Roosevelt,
  Oyster Bay,
    New York.

Dear Colonel Roosevelt:—

I have been thinking very seriously about the relation of our judges to our constitutional system and after considerable study I have tried to make the following rough analysis which I thought I would send to you, hoping that I may get your criticism on it, because I may be called upon to draft something for the Wisconsin Legislature within a year or so and I am trying to get the very best knowledge I can from all sources. . . .

. . . Would it not be well then to divide in some way the proposed recall of judges so that it can be applied directly in some manner whenever the judges have exceeded the constitutional limits laid down by the masters—the people—for them? If the people intended the legislature to legislate and the judges are really doing it, is there not some reason for the recall being applied to cases where the judges have exceeded their authority in usurping the power of the legislature or that of the masters—the people? . . .

I would suggest that some procedures similar to the following might be worked out:

By a majority vote of the legislature it asserts that the judges have usurped legislative function by interpretation or nullification, specifying a particular case and giving a hearing. If the legislature by a majority vote finds that such is the case, then it sets a time after the legislature for an election of the judge. If he is elected, then he is sustained, but if he is not, then an opponent is elected. The people show their disapproval of the courses of the particular judge. Or, we could have a proceeding by which the people could assert through a petition that a judge has usurped legislative function. Then a legislature must give a hearing and follow the above procedure. . . .

Very truly yours,
Charles McCarthy

October 27th, 1911.

My dear Mr. McCarthy:

Your letter interests me particularly because you are evidently thinking along just the lines that I am thinking. In my speeches about the New York judges I am not talking about the men who have committed impeachable offences, and I am talking of some men whom I do not want to recall or take off the Bench. Neither do I wish to give the Legislature the final control over them. But I do most emphatically wish to give *the people* the ultimate right to say what the laws shall be. I believe that two entirely distinct remedies must be achieved. One is in some way or other by majority vote of the Legislature, or in other fashion, to permit a judge to be removed not for an impeachable offence but because the people no longer think him the right kind of public servant. . . . Next, and much more important, I wish in some fashion, perhaps by the use of the initiative in a somewhat analogous way to that which you have devised in Wisconsin as I understand it, that the people shall be allowed to express their judgment on any construction of the Constitution by the judges, and this expression should be final. Of course it could not be final as regards the National Constitution with the people of any State, but it could be final as to any interpretation by the State judges of the State Constitution, or, so far as they are concerned, of the National Constitution, until the latter question had been settled by the National judiciary. . . .

Sincerely yours,
(Signed) Theodore Roosevelt.

6

CHICAGO DAILY TRIBUNE

For Chairman of the Convention

June 18, 1912

This cartoon, which appeared after the Taft forces took control of the Republican National Convention, played upon Roosevelt's dominance in the popular primaries, suggesting that Taft's nomination was an affront to justice and democracy.

Chicago Daily Tribune, June 18, 1912, 3.

7

THEODORE ROOSEVELT

A Confession of Faith

August 6, 1912

In this speech, delivered in Chicago less than two months after he bolted from the Republican convention, Roosevelt accepted the nomination of the newly formed Progressive party. Roosevelt attempted to attract as many supporters as possible, calling for direct democracy, social justice, corporate registration and regulation, women's suffrage, and a host of other social and economic reforms. He equated reform with salvation by entitling his speech "A Confession of Faith" and ending with the exhortation, "We stand at Armageddon, and we battle for the Lord."

To you, men and women who have come here to this great city of this great State formally to launch a new party, a party of the people of the whole Union, the National Progressive party, I extend my hearty greeting. You are taking a bold and a greatly needed step for the service of our beloved country. . . .

The first essential in the Progressive programme is the right of the people to rule. But a few months ago our opponents were assuring us with insincere clamor that it was absurd for us to talk about desiring that the people should rule, because, as a matter of fact, the people actually do rule. Since that time the actions of the Chicago Convention, and to an only less degree of the Baltimore Convention, have shown in striking fashion how little the people do rule under our present conditions.

We should provide by national law for presidential primaries. We should provide for the election of United States senators by popular vote. We should provide for a short ballot; nothing makes it harder for the people to control their public servants than to force them to vote for so many officials that they cannot really keep track of any one of them, so that each becomes indistinguishable in the crowd around him. There must be stringent and efficient corrupt-practices acts,

Theodore Roosevelt, *The Works of Theodore Roosevelt: National Edition,* vol. 17, ed. Hermann Hagedorn (New York: Charles Scribner's Sons, 1926), 254–99.

applying to the primaries as well as the elections; and there should be publicity of campaign contributions during the campaign.

We should provide throughout this Union for giving the people in every State the real right to rule themselves, and really and not nominally to control their public servants and their agencies for doing the public business. . . .

I have not come to this way of thinking from closet study, or as a mere matter of theory; I have been forced to it by a long experience with the actual conditions of our political life. A few years ago, for instance, there was very little demand in this country for presidential primaries. There would have been no demand now if the politicians had really endeavored to carry out the will of the people as regards nominations for President. But, largely under the influence of special privilege in the business world, there have arisen castes of politicians who not only do not represent the people, but who make their bread and butter by thwarting the wishes of the people. This is true of the bosses of both political parties in my own State of New York, and it is just as true of the bosses of one or the other political party in a great many States of the Union. The power of the people must be made supreme within the several party organizations.

In the contest which culminated six weeks ago in this city I speedily found that my chance was at a minimum in any State where I could not get an expression of the people themselves in the primaries. I found that if I could appeal to the rank and file of the Republican voters, I could generally win, whereas, if I had to appeal to the political caste— which includes the most noisy defenders of the old system—I generally lost. Moreover, I found, as a matter of fact, not as a matter of theory, that these politicians habitually and unhesitatingly resort to every species of mean swindling and cheating in order to carry their point. It is because of the general recognition of this fact that the words politics and politicians have grown to have a sinister meaning throughout this country. The bosses and their agents in the National Republican Convention at Chicago treated political theft as a legitimate political weapon. It is instructive to compare the votes of States where there were open primaries and the votes of States where there were not. In Illinois, Pennsylvania, and Ohio we had direct primaries, and the Taft machine was beaten two to one. Between and bordering on these States were Michigan, Indiana, and Kentucky. In these States we could not get direct primaries, and the politicians elected two delegates to our one. . . .

Now, my proposal is merely that we shall give to the people the power, to be used not wantonly but only in exceptional cases, themselves to see to it that the governmental action taken in their name is really the action that they desire.

The American people, and not the courts, are to determine their own fundamental policies. The people should have power to deal with the effect of the acts of all their governmental agencies. This must be extended to include the effects of judicial acts as well as the acts of the executive and legislative representatives of the people. . . .

In the last twenty years an increasing percentage of our people have come to depend on industry for their livelihood, so that to-day the wage-workers in industry rank in importance side by side with the tillers of the soil. As a people we cannot afford to let any group of citizens or any individual citizen live or labor under conditions which are injurious to the common welfare. Industry, therefore, must submit to such public regulation as will make it a means of life and health, not of death or inefficiency. We must protect the crushable elements at the base of our present industrial structure. . . .

Ultimately we desire to use the government to aid, as far as can safely be done, in helping the industrial tool-users to become in part tool-owners, just as our farmers now are. Ultimately the government may have to join more efficiently than at present in strengthening the hands of the working men who already stand at a high level, industrially and socially, and who are able by joint action to serve themselves. But the most pressing and immediate need is to deal with the cases of those who are on the level, and who are not only in need themselves, but because of their need tend to jeopardize the welfare of those who are better off.

We hold that under no industrial order, in no commonwealth, in no trade, and in no establishment should industry be carried on under conditions inimical to the social welfare. The abnormal, ruthless, spendthrift industry of establishment tends to drag down all to the level of the least considerate. . . .

. . . We hold that minimum wage commissions should be established in the nation and in each State to inquire into wages paid in various industries and to determine the standard which the public ought to sanction as a minimum; and we believe that, as a present instalment of what we hope for in the future, there should be at once established in the nation and its several States minimum standards for the wages of women, taking the present Massachusetts law as a basis from which to start and on which to improve. . . .

. . . We stand for the passage of legislation in the nation and in all States providing standards of compensation for industrial accidents and death, and for diseases clearly due to the nature of conditions of industry, and we stand for the adoption by law of a fair standard of compensation for casualties resulting fatally which shall clearly fix the minimum compensation in all cases.

In the third place, certain industrial conditions fall clearly below the levels which the public to-day sanction.

We stand for a living wage. Wages are subnormal if they fail to provide a living for those who devote their time and energy to industrial occupations. The monetary equivalent of a living wage varies according to local conditions, but must include enough to secure the elements of a normal standard of living—a standard high enough to make morality possible, to provide for education and recreation, to care for immature members of the family, to maintain the family during periods of sickness, and to permit of reasonable saving for old age.

Hours are excessive if they fail to afford the worker sufficient time to recuperate and return to his work thoroughly refreshed. We hold that the night labor of women and children is abnormal and should be prohibited; we hold that the employment of women over forty-eight hours per week is abnormal and should be prohibited. We hold that the seven-day working week is abnormal, and we hold that one day of rest in seven should be provided by law. . . .

Safety conditions are abnormal when, through unguarded machinery, poisons, electrical voltage, or otherwise, the workers are subjected to unnecessary hazards of life and limb; and all such occupations should come under governmental regulation and control. . . .

The premature employment of children is abnormal and should be prohibited; so also the employment of women in manufacturing, commerce, or other trades where work compels standing constantly; and also any employment of women in such trades for a period of at least eight weeks at time of childbirth. . . .

Our aim is to control business, not to strangle it—and, above all, not to continue a policy of make-believe strangle toward big concerns that do evil, and constant menace toward both big and little concerns that do well.

Our aim is to promote prosperity, and then see to its proper division. We do not believe that any good comes to any one by a policy which means destruction of prosperity; for in such cases it is not possible to divide it because of the very obvious fact that there is nothing to divide. We wish to control big business so as to secure among other things good wages for the wage-workers and reasonable prices for the consumers. Wherever in any business the prosperity of the business man is obtained by lowering the wages of his workmen and charging an excessive price to the consumers, we wish to interfere and stop such practices. We will not submit to that kind of prosperity any more than we will submit to prosperity obtained by swindling investors or getting unfair advantages over business rivals. . . .

Again and again while I was President, from 1902 to 1908, I pointed out that under the antitrust law alone it was neither possible to put a stop to business abuses nor possible to secure the highest efficiency in the service rendered by business to the general public. The antitrust law must be kept on our statute-books, and, as hereafter shown, must be rendered more effective in the cases where it is applied. But to treat the antitrust law as an adequate, or as by itself a wise, measure of relief and betterment is a sign not of progress, but of Toryism and reaction. It has been of benefit so far as it has implied the recognition of a real and great evil, and the at least sporadic application of the principle that all men alike must obey the law. But as a sole remedy, universally applicable, it has in actual practice completely broken down; as now applied it works more mischief than benefit. . . .

An important volume entitled "Concentration and Control" has just been issued by President Charles R. Van Hise, of the University of Wisconsin.* The University of Wisconsin has been more influential than any other agency in making Wisconsin what it has become, a laboratory for wise social and industrial experiment in the betterment of conditions. President Van Hise is one of those thoroughgoing but sane and intelligent radicals from whom much of leadership is to be expected in such a matter. The subtitle of his book shows that his endeavor is to turn the attention of his countrymen toward practically solving the trust problem of the United States. In his preface he states that his aim is to suggest a way to gain the economic advantages of the concentration of industry and at the same time to guard the interests of the public, and to assist in the rule of enlightenment, reason, fair play, mutual consideration, and toleration. In sum, he shows that unrestrained competition as an economic principle has become too destructive to be permitted to exist and that the small men must be allowed to co-operate under penalty of succumbing before their big competitors; and yet such co-operation, vitally necessary to the small man, is criminal under the present law.

---

*Roosevelt went on to quote Van Hise at length. For an excerpt of Van Hise's book, see Document 12.

It is utterly hopeless to attempt to control the trusts merely by the antitrust law, or by any law the same in principle, no matter what the modifications may be in detail. In the first place, these great corporations cannot possibly be controlled merely by a succession of lawsuits. The administrative branch of the government must exercise such control. . . .

. . . The antitrust law should be kept on the statute-books and strengthened so as to make it genuinely and thoroughly effective against every big concern tending to monopoly or guilty of antisocial practices. At the same time, a national industrial commission should be created which should have complete power to regulate and control all the great industrial concerns engaged in interstate business—which practically means all of them in this country. This commission should exercise over these industrial concerns like powers to those exercised over the railways by the Interstate Commerce Commission. . . .

This commission should deal with all the abuses of the trusts—all the abuses such as those developed by the government suit against the Standard Oil and Tobacco Trusts—as the Interstate Commerce Commission now deals with rebates.* It should have complete power to make the capitalization absolutely honest and put a stop to all stock watering. . . .

. . . It should have power to compel the unsparing publicity of all the acts of any corporation which goes wrong. The regulation should be primarily under the administrative branch of the government, and not by lawsuit. It should prohibit and effectually punish monopoly achieved through wrong, and also actual wrongs done by industrial corporations which are not monopolies, such as the artificial raising of prices, the artificial restriction on productivity, the elimination of competition by unfair or predatory practices, and the like; leaving industrial organizations free within the limits of fair and honest dealing to promote through the inherent efficiency of organization the power of the United States as a competitive nation among nations, and the greater abundance at home that will come to our people from that power wisely exercised.

*In 1911 the Supreme Court had ruled that the American Tobacco Company and Standard Oil were guilty of violating the Sherman Antitrust Act and ordered that the companies be broken up. However, the dissolution took so long that it was ineffective, and the companies remained as powerful as before. Furthermore in setting forth a new standard of "reasonableness" in measuring restraints in trade, the court weakened the Sherman Act at the same time that it broke up the two companies.

Any corporation voluntarily coming under the commission should not be prosecuted under the antitrust law as long as it obeys in good faith the orders of the commission. The commission would be able to interpret in advance, to any honest man asking the interpretation, what he may do and what he may not do in carrying on a legitimate business. Any corporation not coming under the commission should be exposed to prosecution under the antitrust law, and any corporation violating the orders of the commission should also at once become exposed to such prosecution; and when such a prosecution is successful, it should be the duty of the commission to see that the decree of the court is put into effect completely and in good faith, so that the combination is absolutely broken up, and is not allowed to come together again, nor the constituent parts thereof permitted to do business save under the conditions laid down by the commission. This last provision would prevent the repetition of such gross scandals as those attendant upon the present Administration's prosecution of the Standard Oil and the Tobacco Trusts. The Supreme Court of the United States in condemning these two trusts to dissolution used language of unsparing severity concerning their actions. But the decree was carried out in such a manner as to turn into a farce this bitter condemnation of the criminals by the highest court in the country. . . .

We favor co-operation in business, and ask only that it be carried on in a spirit of honesty and fairness. We are against crooked business, big or little. We are in favor of honest business, big or little. We propose to penalize conduct and not size. But all very big business, even though honestly conducted, is fraught with such potentiality of menace that there should be thoroughgoing governmental control over it, so that its efficiency in promoting prosperity at home and increasing the power of the nation in international commerce may be maintained, and at the same time fair play insured to the wage-workers, the small business competitors, the investors, and the general public. Wherever it is practicable we propose to preserve competition; but where under modern conditions competition has been eliminated and cannot be successfully restored, then the government must step in and itself supply the needed control on behalf of the people as a whole. . . .

Now, friends, this is my confession of faith. I have made it rather long because I wish you to know what my deepest convictions are on the great questions of to-day, so that if you choose to make me your standard-bearer in the fight you shall make your choice understanding exactly how I feel. . . . The convictions to which I have come have not been arrived at as the result of study in the closet or the library, but from the knowledge I have gained through hard experience during the many years in which, under many and varied conditions, I have striven and toiled with men. I believe in a larger use of the governmental power to help remedy industrial wrongs, because it has been borne in on me by actual experience that without the exercise of such power many of the wrongs will go unremedied. I believe in a larger opportunity for the people themselves directly to participate in government and to control their governmental agents, because long experience has taught me that without such control many of their agents will represent them badly. . . .

Surely there never was a fight better worth making than the one in which we are engaged. It little matters what befalls any one of us who for the time being stands in the forefront of the battle. I hope we shall win, and I believe that if we can wake the people to what the fight really means we shall win. But, win or lose, we shall not falter. Whatever fate may at the moment overtake any of us, the movement itself will not stop. Our cause is based on the eternal principles of righteousness; and even though we who now lead may for the time fail, in the end the cause itself shall triumph. Six weeks ago, here in Chicago, I spoke to the honest representatives of a convention which was not dominated by honest men; a convention wherein sat, alas! a majority of men who, with sneering indifference to every principle of right, so acted as to bring to a shameful end a party which had been founded over a half-century ago by men in whose souls burned the fire of lofty endeavor. Now to you men, who, in your turn, have come together to spend and be spent in the endless crusade against wrong, to you who face the future resolute and confident, to you who strive in a spirit of brotherhood for the betterment of our nation, to you who gird yourselves for this great new fight in the never-ending warfare for the good of humankind, I say in closing what in that speech I said in closing: We stand at Armageddon, and we battle for the Lord.

8

ST. LOUIS POST DISPATCH

The Senior Partner
September 8, 1912

THE SENIOR PARTNER

Some critics argued that Roosevelt's proposal to create a federal board to regulate corporations would draw the government and big business so close together that they would form a partnership. This cartoon played off such a fear, showing the trusts giving orders to Uncle Sam.

St. Louis Post Dispatch, September 8, 1912, 14.

9

THEODORE ROOSEVELT

Letters to Mary Ella Lyon Swift, Florence Kelley, and Jane Addams

March 7, 1911, January 9, 1912, and ca. August 8, 1912

This correspondence shows the development of Roosevelt's attitude toward women's suffrage from "tepid" to "ferociously intense" support.

Mary Ella Lyon Swift was an opponent of women's suffrage. Florence Kelley was the general secretary for the National Consumers' League, a veteran political activist, and an associate of the settlement house movement. Jane Addams was the cofounder of Hull House, America's most notable settlement house, and a constant voice calling for social justice for men and women, including women's suffrage.

To Mary Ella Lyon Swift

OYSTER BAY, MARCH 7, 1911

My dear Mrs. Swift:

I am interested in those letters about the suffrage that you have written. I am rather in favor of the suffrage, but very tepidly. Women do not really need the suffrage although I do not think they would do any harm with it. Their needs are along entirely different lines, and their duties are along entirely different lines. Indeed, the longer I stay in politics the more I realize for men quite as much as for women, while there are very grave duties connected with politics there are even greater and more important duties either outside of them altogether or only indirectly connected with them.

Faithfully yours

Theodore Roosevelt, *Letters of Theodore Roosevelt,* vol. 7, ed. Elting E. Morrison (Cambridge, Mass.: Harvard University Press, 1954), 240–41, 475, 594–95.

To Florence Kelley

NEW YORK, JANUARY 9, 1912

My dear Miss Kelley:
I have read that book, but I shall reread it. All that is necessary to make me the most ferociously intense believer in woman suffrage instead of its moderate supporter as at present, is to convince me that women will take an effective stand against sexual viciousness, which of course means especially against male sexual viciousness. They did take such a stand in Seattle. They have helped Lindsey in Denver, but I do not think they have done as much as I had hoped in Denver.

I hope you like what I wrote about the judges.

Faithfully yours

To Jane Addams

TELEGRAM

EN ROUTE TO OYSTER BAY, UNDATED

Dear Miss Addams:
I wished to see you in person to thank you for seconding me.* I do it now instead. I prized your action not only because of what you are and stand for, but because of what it symbolized for the new movement. In this great National Convention starting the new party women have thereby been shown to have their place to fill precisely as men have, and on an absolute equality. It is idle now to argue whether women can play their part in politics, because in this convention we saw the accomplished fact, and moreover the women who have actively participated in this work of launching the new party represent all that we are most proud to associate with American womanhood. My earnest hope is to see the Progressive Party movement in all its State and local divisions recognize this fact, precisely as it has been recognized at the National Convention. Our party stands for social and industrial justice, and we have a right to expect that women and men will work within the party for the cause with the same high sincerity of purpose and with like efficiency. I therefore earnestly hope that in the campaign now opened we shall see women active members of the various State and County committees. Four women are to be put on the National Committee, and I trust that there will be a full representation of them on every State and County committee. . . .

*In a historic action, Addams had been the first woman to make a speech supporting the nomination of a presidential candidate at a national political convention.

To Jane Addams

TELEGRAM

EN ROUTE TO OYSTER BAY, UNDATED

Did I put into telegram the flat-footed statement without qualification or equivocation that I was for woman suffrage, that the Progressive Party is for woman suffrage, and that I believe within half a dozen years we shall have no one in the United States against it. If not, please insert this, making it as strong as you can, and also wire me if there is anything further of any kind you wish me to put in.

10

THEODORE ROOSEVELT

Letter to Julian La Rose Harris

August 1, 1912

Julian Harris was the son of author Joel Chandler Harris, a white southerner whose stories of Uncle Remus, an ex-slave, influenced white northerners' views of African Americans and race relations in the post–Civil War South. Julian Harris helped organize southern delegations to the Progressive party convention. Delegations from three southern states (Florida, Georgia, and Mississippi) split on the issue of segregation, and each state sent both an integrated and a "lily-white" delegation. Hoping to gain the votes of white Democrats, the Progressive party Credentials Committee ruled in favor of the all-white delegations. In this letter Roosevelt explained why the Progressives would pursue a policy that favored white delegates in the South.

OYSTER BAY, AUGUST 1, 1912

My dear Mr. Harris:

Many letters dealing with the subject of which you spoke to me have been sent to me within the last few days. These letters, from equally worthy citizens, take diametrically opposite positions. Those written by men living in the North usually ask me to insist that we get from

Theodore Roosevelt, *Letters of Theodore Roosevelt,* vol. 7, ed. Elting E. Morrison (Cambridge, Mass.: Harvard University Press, 1954), 584–90.

the South colored Delegates to the National Progressive Convention. Those written by citizens of the South ask that I declare that the new party shall be a white man's party. I am not able to agree to either proposal. . . .

In many of the States of the Union where there is a considerable colored population we are able in very fact and at the present moment to bring the best colored men into the movement on the same terms as the white man. In Rhode Island and Maryland, in New York and Indiana, in Ohio and Illinois, in New Jersey and Pennsylvania, to speak only of States of which I have personal knowledge, this is now being done, and from some or all of these states colored delegates will be sent to the National Progressive Convention in Chicago. Let me point out that the Progressive Party is already, at its very birth, endeavoring in these States, in its own home, to act with fuller recognition of the rights of the colored man than ever the Republican Party did. . . .

There are other States, including the majority of the Southern States where the conditions are wholly different. . . .

For forty-five years the Republican Party has striven to build up in the Southern States in question a party based on the theory that the pyramid will unsupported stand permanently on its apex instead of on its base. For forty-five years the Republican Party has endeavored in these States to build up a party in which the negro should be dominant, a party consisting almost exclusively of negroes. Those who took the lead in this experiment were actuated by high motives, and no one should now blame them because of what, with the knowledge they then had and under the then existing circumstances, they strove to do. But in actual practice the result has been lamentable from every standpoint. It has been productive of evil to the colored men themselves; it has been productive only of evil to the white men of the South; and it has worked the gravest injury to, and finally the disruption and destruction of, the great Republican Party itself. In the States in question where the negro predominates in numbers, and in the sections of other states in which he predominates in numbers, the Republican Party has in actual fact become practically non-existent in so far as votes at the polls are concerned. The number of votes cast in these states and districts for the Republican ticket on Election Day has become negligible. . . .

The action of the Republican machine in the South, then, in endeavoring to keep alive a party based only on negro votes, where, with few exceptions, the white leaders are in it only to gain reward for themselves by trafficking in negro votes, has been bad for the white men of the South, whom it has kept solidified in an unhealthy and unnatural political bond, to their great detriment and to the detriment of the whole Union; and it has been bad for the colored men of the South. The effect on the Republican Party has long been disastrous, and has finally proved fatal. There has in the past been much venality in Republican National Conventions in which there was an active contest for the nomination for President, and this venality has been almost exclusively among the rotten-borough delegates, and for the most part among the negro delegates from these Southern States in which there was no real Republican Party. Finally, in the Convention at Chicago last June, the breakup of the Republican Party was forced by those rotten-borough delegates from the South. In the Primary States of the North the colored men in most places voted substantially as their white neighbors voted. But in the Southern States, where there was no real Republican Party, and where colored men, or whites selected purely by colored men, were sent to the convention, representing nothing but their own greed for money or office the majority was overwhelmingly antiprogressive. Seven eighths of the colored men from these rotten-borough districts upheld by their votes the fraudulent actions of the men who in that Convention defied and betrayed the will of the mass of the plain people of the party. In spite of the hand-picked delegates chosen by the bosses in certain northern states, in spite of the scores of delegates deliberately stolen from the rank and file of the party by the corrupt political machine which dominated the National Committee and the Convention itself, there would yet have been no hope of reversing in the National Convention the action demanded by the overwhelming majority of the Republicans who had a chance to speak for themselves in their primaries, had it not been for the two hundred and fifty votes or thereabouts sent from the states in which there is no Republican Party. For forty-five years everything has been sacrificed to the effort to build up in these states a Republican Party which should be predominantly and overwhelmingly negro, and now those for whom the effort has been made turned and betrayed that party itself.... The loss of instant representation by Southern colored delegates is due to the fact that the sentiment of the Southern negro collectively has been prostituted by dishonest professional politicians both white and black, and the machinery does not exist (and can never be created as long as present political conditions are continued) which can secure what a future of real justice will undoubtedly develop, namely, the right of political expression by the negro who shows that he possesses the intelligence, integrity and self-respect which justify such right of political expression in his white neighbor.

...I earnestly believe that by appealing to the best white men in the South, the men of justice and of vision as well as of strength and leadership, and by frankly putting the movement in their hands from the outset we shall create a situation by which the colored men of the South will ultimately get justice as it is not possible for them to get justice if we are to continue and perpetuate the present conditions. The men to whom we appeal are the men who have stood for securing the colored man in his rights before the law, and they can do for him what neither the Northern white man nor the colored men themselves can do. Our only wise course from the standpoint of the colored man himself is to follow the course that we are following toward him in the North and to follow the course we are following toward him in the South.

Very truly yours

11

CHARLES VAN HISE

Letters to Senator Robert M. La Follette
October 30, 1911, and November 21, 1911

In these letters Van Hise tried to convince La Follette that the federal government should attempt to control rather than destroy large-scale corporations. Van Hise and La Follette were classmates at the University of Wisconsin and remained friends through 1912. Although Van Hise failed to convert La Follette to his position, the letters reveal the political and legal implications of the procorporate position more clearly. In writing to La Follette, Van Hise explicitly rejected the idea that laws could be used to limit corporate power, telling him, "You should be a leader in the movement for concentration, cooperation, and control, and should set yourself squarely against attempting to control the flood tide of economic tendency by further restrictive statute legislation." (See Document 10.)

Charles Van Hise, Letters to Robert M. La Follette, *La Follette Family Papers,* Manuscripts Division, Library of Congress, series B, boxes 70 and 72.

OCTOBER 30, 1911.

My dear Robert:

During the month that I have been home I have been trying to get hold of what happened during the summer and the trend of affairs. As to the former I have found your magazine the most helpful of any publication. On the latter point I should like to make to you one suggestion. It is this, that you and the group with which you are associated do nothing to prevent your taking the position in the future that the proper solution in reference to great aggregations of wealth is by control rather than by disintegration. While perhaps I do not fully comprehend your amendment to the Sherman Law I suspect you have this in mind, in which case this part of my letter need not have been written.

From the point of view of conservation, the great aggregations of wealth, such as the U.S. Steel Corporation, the coupling up of water powers in the same districts, etc., result in great economic advantage not only in conservative use of a material but in economic efficiency. Some arrangement should be made by which aggregation is allowed to go to the extent that there will be increased economy and efficiency. If the U.S. Steel Corporation is found to have violated the Sherman Law and it is therefore destroyed, I have no doubt that this will be a disadvantage rather than an advantage to the people. . . .

Very truly yours,
Charles R. Van Hise

NOVEMBER 21, 1911.

My dear Robert:

On my way home I thought much of the discussion we had on Sunday, and especially of the position which Mr. Brandeis takes as to the possibility of returning to competition to regulate aggregations in industry. In this letter I shall not attempt to present further my arguments to meet his points, but merely say that I suspect that Mr. Brandeis is too much influenced by his experience in law practice; that he has not sufficiently considered the problem from the broadest point of view.

To the assumptions he makes as to the advantage of competition and the further assumptions that similar advantages cannot be obtained with concentration I object in each case, and as a result of conference I believe he will not gain support for his views among sound economists.

It seems to me that in the long run great economic advantage if properly regulated and the gains distributed is likely to lead to social advantage. He who takes a contrary position has a difficult one to defend. . . .

Remembering our visit with great pleasure, I am,

Very sincerely yours,
Charles R. Van Hise

12

THEODORE ROOSEVELT

Letter to Charles R. Van Hise
June 4, 1912

and

CHARLES R. VAN HISE

From Concentration and Control
1912

Roosevelt's letter suggests his interest in Van Hise's ideas, an interest evidenced by Roosevelt's extensive quotation from Van Hise in his "Confession of Faith" speech. (See Document 7.)

The excerpt from Concentration and Control *shows that Van Hise's main concern was that the government create the conditions necessary to allow for the "highest economic efficiency," conditions that explicitly included massive size ("sufficient magnitude") and repudiation of competition—the key to laissez-faire social and economic policy. (See also Document 11.) Van Hise's emphasis was slightly different from Roosevelt's, but the similarity of their goals and assumptions illustrates the potential power and procorporate radicalism inherent in Roosevelt's program. Roosevelt emphasized the regulatory aspects of the national government, whereas Van Hise chose the more benign idea of cooperation and coordi-*

Charles R. Van Hise, *Concentration and Control: A Solution of the Trust Problem in the United States* (New York: Macmillan, 1912), 8–10, 14, 17, 100, 226–27, 232.

nation; regardless of the nuances of terminology, they held a common position that saw the power of organized wealth as inevitable, positive, and necessarily subject to the control of federal authorities.

Letter to Charles Van Hise

JUNE 4TH, 1912.

My dear President Van Hise:
I am really obliged to you for the advance sheets of your book. Though I am worked to death, I shall take it up and read it at once.

Faithfully yours,
T. Roosevelt

Charles R. Van Hise, from *Concentration and Control*

What are the economic advantages of manufacturing in a large plant and doing business on a large scale, and how important are they? Different industries differ among themselves very greatly in these respects, and any general statement will need modification when applied to a particular case. What is said will be more applicable to those groups of industries which are better adapted for concentration.

The Handling of Material. —The handling of material on a large scale in itself gives great economy. In any manufactory the material must be there assembled. For instance, if it be an iron manufactory, and we have a primitive bloomery depending upon an adjacent bank of ore, it will not pay to go to any great expense in providing for transportation of the ore to the bloomery; and the ore will be hauled in a cart. When the bloomery changes to the blast furnace, the quantity of ore needed will be so great that the ore is brought with trams or some kind of mechanical haulage. The same is true of the coal. Thus the economics due to mere magnitude of operation in this industry become very great. Also in the manufacturing process itself the large furnace has an advantage in economy of fuel and efficiency over the small furnace. . . .

Subdivision of Labor. —In most manufactories an article must go through many processes before it is completed. In the old primitive shop, the shoemaker at the bench did all of the different stages of work in making the entire shoe. In the large manufactory the part that any one man does has been steadily lessened until now in the making of a single shoe many persons participate. In the making of a wagon or a binder in a large manufactory scores of people take part. In the wagon shop which served the country community one man, or one man with his helper, made the wagon in all its parts except that the iron in bars or rods was furnished to him. Specialization of labor is only possible in the large manufactory, and it is generally agreed that such specialization gives increased efficiency.

Integration. —A further step in the development of concentration of industry is its integration; that is, a corporation handles not one stage of manufacture only, but a number or even all of the stages from the raw material to the finished product. This again gives increased economy and efficiency, because all the different units of the integrated industry are in harmony, one with reference to the other. . . .

Business Advantages of Concentration. —Thus far the industrial advantages of concentration only have been given. Upon the business side there are also great economies. Some of the more important of these are as follows: —

(*a*) Big organizations are able to buy in large quantities and thus gain the advantages of the lowest rates of purchase.

(*b*) Big organizations are able to sell in large quantities and most advantageously. A large part of the cost of business under new conditions is the marketing of products. In the marketing there are great costs in commercial travelers, in advertisements, etc. . . . With the large concentration the advertising cost per unit of sale is much lower than with the small industry. . . .

Total Advantages of Concentration. —It is not easy to give the economic advantages in terms of percentages for any industry which result from the large factory, the subdivision of labor, the full use of mechanical appliances, the specialization of departments, integration, utilization of by-products, entrance into allied industries, distribution of plants of the same kind, using only the most efficient plants, maintenance of investigating departments, economics of business management, and reduction of amount of capital; but it is safe to say that the gain is very great for the large concentration as compared with the small plant. . . .

The fierceness of modern competition is the inevitable result of the development of transportation and communication. Until these were in a highly advanced condition it was not possible for an organization to reach a great territory with its products. With highly efficient transportation and communication the strong organizations, even if far apart, meet one another in the wide markets; and the destructive struggle is inevitable unless they coöperate. . . .

With the alternative before the business men of coöperation or failure, we may be sure that they will coöperate. Since the law is violated by practically every group of men engaged in trade from one end of the country to the other, they do not feel that in combining they are doing a moral wrong. . . .

Reasonable coöperation between corporations should be permitted. It is believed that in business under modern conditions, coöperation not competition should be the controlling word. Sufficient coöperation should be allowed to prevent fierce and unrestrained competition which goes to the extent of reducing prices below a reasonable amount. Only by coöperation can the enormous wastes of competition be avoided. . . .

Just as coöperation of capital should be allowed, so coöperation of laborers should be permitted. The laborers find themselves prevented from coöperation by the Sherman Law precisely as have the industrial combinations. It is clear that unless laborers may unite in trade unions, in joint bargaining, and in all legitimate matters which concern them, they will be helpless. Not only should coöperation between capitalists and coöperation of laborers be allowed, but coöperation of the two groups should be permitted. In short, it is advocated that the principle of coöperation should control in commerce, including both laborer and capitalist.

Corporations should be allowed to be of sufficient magnitude to give the highest economic efficiency in order that (*a*) they may be able to supply the needs of our own people at the lowest practicable rate, and (*b*) to secure an increased proportion of foreign trade. . . .

. . . we must now accept for this country the principle of coöperation in business. Even the most ardent defender of the competitive system says that competition must be regulated; and he says that the alternative is between regulated competition and regulated monopoly. The writer holds that there is no such alternative. We should not accept competition as the controlling principle on one side, nor monopoly as the controlling principle on the other side. We should accept the broad principle that reasonable coöperation should be allowed in business as it is allowed everywhere else in our social structure.

5

The Anticorporatists:
Robert M. La Follette, Louis D. Brandeis,
and Woodrow Wilson

13

ROBERT M. LA FOLLETTE

Speech at Jamestown, North Dakota
March 14, 1912

La Follette delivered this speech just days before the United States' first presidential primary election, which was held in North Dakota on March 20, 1912. La Follette easily won the primary, gaining more than 57 percent of the vote. In this speech La Follette focused on the power of direct democracy—bringing the citizen and the public official "face to face" to allow the citizen to "point the way he [the politician] should go."

. . . A great power has grown up in this country; so great that men are asking whether it is stronger than the government; whether it is stronger than 90,000,000 of people. It reaches out into national conventions; it controls State conventions; it controls the organization of legislative bodies; it appoints speakers; it determines chairmanships of all important committees; it designates the members of these committees; it frames and shapes all important legislation; it has wrested the government from the people. It is changing the government of the

Robert M. La Follette, speech at Jamestown, North Dakota, *La Follette Family Papers*, Manuscripts Division, Library of Congress, series B, box 215.

fathers. We have the form of the government just as they made it for us, but the soul, the life, of representative [government] is fast being lost to the people of this country. What does it matter if you have the ballot, if that ballot does not insure representative government? Our fathers thought it would be sufficient to give to every citizen the right to vote, but we have learned in the beginning of this 20th century that the ballot will not give to each citizen an equal opportunity; that it does not give to every citizen his representation in the making and execution of the laws. And there is a demand for that reason all over this country, in every state in the Union, for something that will give effectiveness, that will make this ballot,—which in the beginning was believed to be sufficient,—powerful enough to give to the people representative government. So there has grown up everywhere a demand for new instruments to insure democracy to the people,—the initiative, the referendum, the recall, the direct election of United States Senators by the people, the choice of Presidential candidates by direct vote of the people. These instruments of democracy are not designed to change the form of the government. It is not intended that they shall supplant and do away with representative government, but that they shall make government more representative. It has been said by at least one candidate upon the Republican ticket for the Presidency that he favors the initiative and referendum in the respective states; and that he favors some form of a recall. If the initiative, referendum and recall are good for North Dakota, in order to make your state government representative, why are they not good nationally to make your national government representative? . . .

As a progressive, I stand for the initiative, the referendum and the recall as applied to all legislation and as applied to all public officials,—including the judiciary, in each and every state in this Union, and I stand for their broad application nationally as well. I stand for the election of United States Senators by direct vote of the people; for the nomination of all candidates by direct vote of the people, including all officers from President to coroner. And I believe that all this machinery devised by the politicians which has been erected between the citizen and the official should be torn down and thrown onto the political scrap heap; and that the official and the citizen should be brought face to face so that the citizen may lay his hand on the public official, his servant, and point the way he should go. Then we shall have just the kind of government that our fathers designed for us in the beginning. . . .

14

ROBERT M. LA FOLLETTE

Speech at Bismarck, North Dakota

March 14, 1912

This speech contains La Follette's clearest anticorporate statements, including his explanation of how "a mighty power" had grown large enough that it had the potential to control American economic, social, and political life. This speech also includes La Follette's solution, based on the Sherman Act: dissolving large-scale corporations.

. . . I submit to you, my friends of North Dakota, that there has grown up in this country of ours within the last dozen or fifteen years a mighty power, stronger than ever assailed democracy in all the history of the world; a power great enough to name presidential candidates, control national conventions, write national platforms, organize the United States Senate, the House of Representatives, elect the speaker and the chairmen of important committees. It doesn't stop with the exercise of complete political power. It has reached out and taken possession of every line of business in this country. It has laid its hands upon the transportation companies of this great country, controlling the lines that lead to market. Without them that which you produce in this fertile state is absolutely worthless. The control of the highways that lead to markets is the control of the country. And this mighty power that exercises such a potential influence upon the government on the political side exercises a complete influence upon the business, the economic life of the American people, the industrial life of the American people.

It laid its hand upon the transportation companies, and out of 2,000 competing railroads they formed six systems, breaking down all competition. They gathered that together, and when they had finished their work a few years ago we had in this country six great railway systems controlled by eight men, and in that control Morgan and

---

Robert M. La Follette, speech at Bismarck, North Dakota, *La Follette Family Papers,* Manuscripts Division, Library of Congress, series B, box 215.

Rockefeller were dominant. When they destroyed competition, when they brought all of these competing roads under practically one control, then it was that the transportation rates began to amount higher and higher. Reports of the Interstate Commerce Commission show that they increased some years as much as $100,000,000 in a single year. If you would know one thing that has contributed immensely to the great burden that rests upon the American people, represented by what we call high cost of living, look to these increased, and steadily increasing railway transportation charges. That is a part of it. They did not stop with consolidation of transportation lines. About the same time they began an organized consolidation of manufacturing. They brought together all the plants engaged in the manufacture of leather, and the[y] organized the leather trust or combination; they brought together all of the plants, or enough of them to control the manufacture of cottons, and that constituted the cotton trust. . . . Finally, there was no line of business that was any longer competitive. . . . A great statesman, John Sherman of Ohio, in 1890 had seen the thing in the far distance,—a speck on the horizon. And he framed the Sherman Anti-Trust bill and introduced it in the United States Senate in that year. . . . And so the Sherman Law was written upon the statute books of 1890.* At that time there were but few organizations in this country that would be called trusts. You could number them on the fingers of a single hand. But by 1897 there were indications of the formation of a score of them. . . .

Between 1897 and 1900, in three short years, 149 of these combinations were formed with a capitalization of $3,784,000,000; and then it was that the prices,—the cost of living began to increase. If you kept books at that time, and will look up your accounts you will see that prices began to advance in 1897-8-9, and by 1900 the people were beginning to feel those increased prices as a considerable burden upon them. Then it was that they began to clamor for tariff revision,— to get these duties down. They realized that these trusts were fixing prices, and that they were bringing together all of the competitors in an agreement that [there] should be no competition, and that they should name the prices that the American consumer should pay for every article which they produced.

*The Sherman Act was the federal government's main means of limiting the power of large business organizations. The law's declaration that "Every . . . combination . . . in restraint of trade . . . is hereby declared illegal," seemed to give the government clear power over corporate mergers, but in practice the law had limited impact on the increasing power of large corporations.

By 1904 what had happened? 149 trusts and combinations, with a capitalization of $3,784,000,000 in 1900; come down to 1904 and what were the conditions? 8664 great plants theretofore competitive had been brought into these unlawful agreements and combinations, violating the Sherman Anti-Trust Law, behind this tariff wall which excluded and shut out foreign competition, so that they could prey upon the American people at will. . . .

Now I am going to give to former President Roosevelt everything to which he is entitled; but I am going to say to you that I believe that the President of the United States in 1901-2-3 any of those years, when the manifestations of the growth of the trusts were so plain to all the people,—if he had summoned all of the United States district attorneys (over whose tenure of office he had absolute control) to his office in the White House; if he had at the same time summoned the member of his cabinet who presided over the Department of Justice— If you will just permit me to say it, that is what I would have done if I had been President. When these officials were gathered there, I would have had a messenger put into the hands of each one of them a copy of the Sherman Anti-Trust Law; and I would have said to them, "Gentlemen I want you to take this document to your rooms and study it for twenty-four hours, and then come back here to this office tomorrow at this same hour." And when they came back the next day I would have reminded them that there was written in that law,—and it isn't often that you find it in a criminal statute,—a legislative declaration that it was the duty of the government to prosecute violations of that particular statute. . . .

And I am thinking that if that had been done promptly at that time that there would have been in the pockets of the American people this minute hundreds of millions of dollars taken out of the 90,000,000 people of this country in the extortionate charges which these trusts have been able to impose upon the consumers of this nation. . . .

15

THEODORE ROOSEVELT

Letter to Senator Jonathan Bourne
January 2, 1911

Jonathan Bourne was a Republican senator from Oregon who came out against Taft and helped form the main organization to oppose Taft's renomination: the National Progressive Republican League (NPRL). In the summer of 1911 La Follette announced his intention to challenge Taft for the Republican presidential nomination. In this letter Roosevelt explained why he would not join the NPRL and outlined his understanding of direct democracy.

My dear Senator Bourne:
Will you show this letter to Senator La Follette? I am greatly interested in your plan. I entirely agree with you that popular government is fundamental to all other questions. With your five propositions I am also in accord excepting as to (4) I think there should be carefully guarded limitations. [The recall] ... ought to be used with great caution even in those cases where it can be used, and therefore it should not be made easy to apply it; and careful steps should be taken against involving it wantonly or with levity. In the same way, while I believe in the referendum, and more tepidly in the initiative, I think that the value of both will depend upon the comparative infrequency of their use, and that care should be taken to prevent their being invoked unless there is very real demand for them. Again I am not prepared to say whether it would be advisable or indeed possible to use them wisely on a national scale at this time. ...

... Don't forget that the Direct Primary, the Referendum, the direct nomination of senators, etc. are all merely means to ends. On the other hand such legislation as railroad legislation, the physical valuation of railroads, the great bulk of what has been done in the state of Wisconsin, the workmen's compensation act in New York, much that

Theodore Roosevelt, Letter to Jonathan Bourne, *La Follette Family Papers,* Manuscripts Division, Library of Congress, series B, box 70.

has been done in New Jersey under Governor Fort etc. etc. all represent not merely means but ends. . . .

. . . With my present knowledge, while I am entirely in sympathy with the purposes set forth in your letter, I am doubtful whether the particular form you propose is wise. For example last fall, Senator Cummins told me that he personally, and he believes the state of Iowa, were opposed to the Initiative and Referendum, and so far as the initiative is concerned were very strongly opposed to it. Now, I certainly think we ought to find out how Cummins feels, and not only that, but as a matter of expediency, we should find out what the attitude in Iowa is before we split up the progressive forces. The progressives can only win if they carry the moderates with them. . . .

Faithfully yours,
Theodore Roosevelt.

16

GILBERT ROE

Letter to Blanche Morse
March 28, 1912

In this letter Gilbert Roe, La Follette's attorney, friend, and political adviser, drew a distinction between La Follette and Roosevelt by focusing on La Follette's longtime support for women's suffrage. La Follette's wife, Belle, and his daughter, Fola, were both active in suffrage campaigns in Wisconsin and across the nation.

MARCH 28, 1912.

Dear Madam:
I write you at the suggestion of our mutual friend, Mrs. Greely, of this City, concerning the candidacy of Senator La Follette for the republican presidential nomination. It seems to us that this is a great oppor-

Gilbert Roe, Letter to Blanche Morse, *La Follette Family Papers,* Manuscripts Division, Library of Congress, series H, box 4.

tunity for the women of California to help the cause of suffrage all over the country. The contest in California is between Senator La Follette, Colonel Roosevelt, and President Taft. Senator La Follette alone, is the only one that has been and now is consistently for woman suffrage in every state in the union. Mr. Taft has, as you know, pronounced against it; while Colonel Roosevelt is talking such nonsense as submitting it to a referendum vote of the women, and is obviously unwilling to shoulder the responsibility of either supporting it or opposing it. Senator La Follette was for years an advocate of woman suffrage in Wisconsin, and has advocated it throughout his service in the United States Senate, and has always been ready to speak for it on the floor of the Senate, and has worked for it in all honorable ways. . . .

Yours very truly,
Gilbert Roe

17

ST. LOUIS POST DISPATCH

The Only Way
September 17, 1912

and

Pay Day
September 7, 1912

THE ONLY WAY.

These two cartoons illustrate central issues in the 1912 election. In particular, they reflect the anticorporate position that popular political power was the sole means of destroying the trusts and that large corporations such as Standard Oil were so powerful that they could influence everyone, including presidential candidates.

PAY DAY.

18

LOUIS D. BRANDEIS

Letter to Norman Hapgood

July 3, 1912

Norman Hapgood was the publisher of Collier's Magazine, *a leading progressive magazine in which Brandeis published a number of articles, including a critique of Roosevelt's economic program, entitled "Trusts, Efficiency, and the New Party." (See Document 22.) In this letter to Hapgood, written just after the Democratic convention, Brandeis began to consider what Wilson had to offer as a candidate. Brandeis had supported La Follette in the primary campaign, but after Taft was nominated, Brandeis attempted to get La Follette to support Wilson.*

My dear Norman:

I have longed very much for the opportunity of talking over the political situation and other matters with you.

The action of the Baltimore Convention, the masterful and masterly handling of it by Mr. Bryan, should, it seems to me, solve in large part the doubts of the Progressives. I have never met or even seen Wilson, but all that I have heard of him and particularly his discussion of economic problems makes me believe that he possesses certain qualities indispensable to the solution of our problems. The Democrats have certainly done all that is possible now towards purifying the party, through the selection of their candidates, the adoption of their platform and an attempt to drive the money-lenders out of the temple.

It seems to me that it is the duty of the Progressives who do not feel themselves closely bound by party affiliations to give Wilson the fullest possible support, not only to secure his election, but in order to aid him in the very difficult task of carrying out the Progressive policies. . . .

This morning's paper announces that T.R. is determined to go on with the Progressive party in spite of the Baltimore Convention. I

Louis D. Brandeis, *Letters of Louis D. Brandeis*, vol. 2, ed. Melvin I. Urofsky and David W. Levy (Albany: State University of New York Press, 1972), 633–34.

hope he will conclude, instead, to throw to Wilson the support of his Progressive followers. He could have a wonderful influence in that way, and, in that way, there would be some chance of uniting the Progressives,—Democrats, LaFollette men, Rooseveltians, and there would be a chance of securing even some of the Taft Progressives. I am afraid that if T.R. insists upon proceeding with his party he will imperil the success of the Progressives. . . .

Very cordially yours

19

LOUIS D. BRANDEIS

Letter to Alfred Brandeis
August 28, 1912

On August 28, 1912, Brandeis met with Wilson to discuss economic and political ideas.

Dear [Al]: . . .

[Charles R.] Crane telegraphed me Monday Gov. Wilson wanted to see me. So I went to N.Y. & Sea Girt (leaving here Tuesday P.M.)—breakfasted at the Albermarle Hotel (just opposite Democratic Headquarters) (Old Fifth Ave. Hotel)—passed Long Branch on the way to Sea Girt.* I had gone to N.Y. via the Fall River line so passed by Newport.

Was very favorably impressed with Wilson. He is strong, simple, serious, openminded, eager to learn and deliberate. . . .

*Wilson had a summer home in Sea Girt, New Jersey.

Louis D. Brandeis, *Letters of Louis D. Brandeis,* vol. 2, ed. Melvin I. Urofsky and David W. Levy (Albany: State University of New York Press, 1972), 660–61.

20

WOODROW WILSON AND LOUIS D. BRANDEIS

Correspondence

September 27, 1912, and September 30, 1912

At Wilson's request, Brandeis set out a detailed economic and political vision, drawing heavily on his previous work with La Follette. The material Brandeis provided helped shape Wilson's ideas in the last month of the campaign.

Telegram to Louis Brandeis

HARTFORD, CONN SEPT. 27, [19]12

Please set forth as explicitly as possible the actual measures by which competition can be effectively regulated. The more explicit we are on this point, the more completely will the enemies guns be spiked.

Woodrow Wilson

Letter to Woodrow Wilson

SEPT. 30, 1912. L.D.B.

SUGGESTIONS FOR LETTER OF GOVERNOR WILSON ON TRUSTS.

You have asked me to state what the essential difference is between the Democratic Party's solution of the Trust Problem and that of the New Party; and how we propose to "regulate competition."

My answer is this:

The two parties differ fundamentally regarding the economic policy which the country should pursue. The Democratic Party insists that competition can be and should be maintained in every branch of private industry; that competition can be and should be restored in those branches of industry in which it has been suppressed by the trusts; and that, if at any future time monopoly should appear to be desirable in any

Papers of Woodrow Wilson, vol. 25, ed. Arthur S. Link (Princeton, N.J.: Princeton University Press, 1978), 272, 286–304.

branch of industry, the monopoly should be a public one—a monopoly owned by the people and not by the capitalists. The New Party, on the other hand, insists that private monopoly may be desirable in some branches of industry, or at all events, *is* inevitable; and that existing trusts should not be dismembered or forcibly dislodged from those branches of industry in which they have already acquired a monopoly, but should be made "good" by regulation. In other words, the New Party declares that private monopoly in industry is not necessarily evil, but may do evil; and that legislation should be limited to such *laws and regulations* as should attempt merely to prevent the doing of evil. The New Party does not fear commercial power, however great, if only methods for regulation are provided. We believe that no methods of regulation ever have been or can be devised to remove the menace inherent in private monopoly and overweening commercial power.

This difference in the economic policy of the two parties is fundamental and irreconcilable. . . .

The Sherman Anti Trust Act has, in the past, been little more than a declaration of our economic policy. The experience gained in the twenty-two years since the Act was passed has, however, served some useful purpose. It has established the soundness of the economic policy which it embodies; and it has taught us what the defects in the statute are which have in large part prevented its effective operation. To make that Sherman Law a controlling force,—to preserve competition where it now exists, and to restore competition where it has been suppressed,—additional and comprehensive legislation is necessary. The prohibitions upon combination contained in the act must be made more definite; the provisions for enforcing its provisions by the Courts must be improved; and they must be supplemented by other adequate machinery to be administered by a Federal Board or Commission.

The general character of this new legislation should be as follows:

First: Remove the Uncertainties in the Sherman Law.

This can be accomplished, in large measure, by making the prohibitions upon combination more definite somewhat as the La Follette-Stanley Anti Trust bills propose. The Sherman Law, as interpreted by the United States Supreme Court, prohibits monopolies and combinations "unreasonably" in restraint of trade. Experience has taught us, in the main, what combinations are thus "unreasonable." They are the combinations which suppress competition. And experience has also taught us that competition is never suppressed by the greater efficiency of one concern. It is suppressed either by agreement to form a monopoly or by those excesses of competition which are designed to crush a rival. And experience has taught us, likewise, many of the specific methods or means by which the great trusts, utilizing their huge resources or particularly favored positions commonly crush rivals; for instance "cut throat" competition; discrimination against customers who would not deal exclusively with the combination; excluding competitors from access to essential raw material; espionage; doing business under false names; or "fake independents"; securing unfair advantage through railroad rebates; or acquiring, otherwise than through efficiency, such a control over the market as to dominate the trade. . . .

Second: Facilitate the Enforcement of the law by the Courts.

A great advance in regulating competition and preventing monopoly will result from making the judicial machinery efficient. . . . Efficient judicial machinery will give relief to the people by effecting a real disintegration of those trusts which have heretofore suppressed competition and will also enable individuals who have suffered from illegal acts to secure adequate compensation. . . .

Third: Create a Board or Commission to Aid in Administering the Sherman Law.

The functions of government should not be limited to the enactment of wise rules of action, and the providing of efficient judicial machinery, by which those guilty of breaking the law may be punished, and those injured, secure compensation. The Government, at least where the general public is concerned, is charged with securing also compliance with the law. We need the inspector and the policeman, even more than we need the prosecuting attorney; and we need for the enforcement of the Sherman Law and regulation of competition an administrative Board with broad powers. What the precise powers of such a Board should be is a subject which will require the most careful consideration of Congress. . . .

21

LOUIS D. BRANDEIS

Letter to Arthur Norman Holcombe

September 11, 1912

Responding to a letter from Arthur Norman Holcombe, a professor of political science at Harvard University and one of Brandeis's professional associates, Brandeis drew a distinction between his ideas and the procorporate position, arguing that it was better to preserve competition than simply try to "mitigate the evils of . . . monopoly."

SEPTEMBER 11, 1912 BOSTON, MASS.

My dear Holcombe:
. . . Your statement that I raise "an unnecessary, undesirable controversy" by differentiating between regulation of competition and regulation of monopoly, assures me that I have been misunderstood, because the distinction, as I regard it, is as fundamental as that between Democracy and Absolutism. It is not a question of whether we shall regulate or not, nor is it a question as to the exact power that may be given to the regulating body. The question is: To what end shall we regulate? In other words, shall we regulate in order to preserve competition and make it beneficent or shall we regulate to mitigate the evils of private monopoly? . . .

Louis D. Brandeis, *Letters of Louis D. Brandeis,* vol. 2, ed. Melvin I. Urofsky and David W. Levy (Albany: State University of New York Press, 1972), 670–71.

22

LOUIS D. BRANDEIS

Trusts, Efficiency, and the New Party

September 14, 1912

In this Collier's Magazine *article and a letter to the magazine's publisher, Brandeis continued his criticisms of the procorporate position. Both Brandeis's critique of procorporate ideas and his own program stemmed from the basic conviction that corporations grew large only by unfairly controlling markets. It is worth noting the connection between Brandeis's critique and Wilson's speeches.*

Leaders of the new party argue that industrial monopolies should be legalized, lest we lose the efficiency of large-scale production and distribution. No argument could be more misleading. The issue of competition *versus* monopoly presents no such alternative as "Shall we have small concerns or large?" "Shall we have ill-equipped plants or well-equipped?" . . .

The history of American trusts . . . shows:

First—No conspicuous American trust owes its existence to the desire for increased efficiency. "Expected economies from combination" figure largely in promoters' prospectuses; but they have never been a compelling motive in the formation of any trust. On the contrary, the purpose of combining has often been to curb efficiency or even to preserve inefficiency, thus frustrating the natural law of survival of the fittest.

Second—No conspicuously profitable trust owes its profits largely to superior efficiency. Some trusts have been very efficient, as have some independent concerns; but conspicuous profits have been secured mainly through control of the market—through the power of monopoly to fix prices—through this exercise of the taxing power.

Third—No conspicuous trust has been efficient enough to maintain long as against the independents its proportion of the business of

Louis D. Brandeis, "Trusts, Efficiency, and the New Party," *Collier's Magazine,* September 14, 1912, 14–15.

the country without continuing to buy up, from time to time, its successful competitors.

These three propositions are, also, true of most of the lesser trusts. If there is any exception, the explanation will, doubtless, be found in extraordinary ability on the part of the managers or unusual trade conditions.

And this further proposition may be added:

Fourth—Most of the trusts which did not secure monopolistic position have failed to show marked success or efficiency, as compared with independent competing concerns.

The Elimination of Efficient Andrew Carnegie

The first proposition is strikingly illustrated by the history of the Steel Trust. The main purpose in forming that trust was to eliminate from the steel business the most efficient manufacturer the world has ever known—Andrew Carnegie. The huge price paid for his company was merely the bribe required to induce him to refrain from exercising his extraordinary ability to make steel cheaply.* Carnegie could make and sell steel several dollars a ton cheaper than any other concern. Because his competitors were unable to rise to his remarkable efficiency, his business career was killed; and the American people were deprived of his ability—his genius—to produce steel cheaply. As the Stanley Investigating Committee found, the acquisition of the Carnegie Company by the promoters of the Steel Trust was "*not the purchase of a mill, but the retirement of a man.*" . . .

Even the Standard Oil Trust, which relied mainly upon its control of the transportation systems and other methods of unfair competition to crush competitors, is shown by Commissioner Smith to have been unable to quite maintain its relative position in the market, despite its continued buying up of competitors.

Of the truth of the fourth proposition, stated above—that most of the trusts which did not secure monopolistic positions have failed to show marked success or efficiency as compared with the independent competing concerns—every reader familiar with business must be able to supply evidence. . . .

---

*By reinvesting profits in the most efficient equipment, Andrew Carnegie had made Carnegie Steel the most powerful steel producer in the United States in the late nineteenth century. In 1901 Carnegie sold his company to an investment group organized by banker J. P. Morgan, which combined Carnegie Steel with a number of other companies to create the giant United States Steel Corporation.

Efficient or inefficient, every company which controls the market is a "money maker." No, the issue of "Competition *versus* Monopoly" cannot be distorted into the issue of "Small Concerns *versus* Large." The unit in business may, of course, be too small to be efficient, and the larger unit has been a common incident of monopoly. But a unit too small for efficiency is by no means a necessary incident of competition. And a unit *too large* to be efficient is no uncommon incident of monopoly. Man's work often outruns the capacity of the individual man; and no matter how good the organization, the capacity of an individual man usually determines the success or failure of a particular enterprise—not only financially to the owners but in service to the community. . . .

23

WOODROW WILSON

Speech at Buffalo, New York
September 2, 1912

Wilson delivered this speech to a working-class audience on Labor Day at the start of his national campaign. He tied the interests of the "working-man" or "wage earner" to the broader interests of the country as a whole. In later portions of the speech he focused more on critiquing Roosevelt's program than providing a specific solution of his own.

Mr. Chairman and fellow citizens:
. . . Why is it that the people of this country are in danger of being discontented with the parties that have pretended to serve them? It [is] because in too many instances their promises were not matched by their performances and men began to say to themselves, "What is the use [of] going to the polls and voting? Nothing happens after the election." Is there any man within the hearing of my voice who can challenge the statement that any party that has forfeited the public confidence, has forfeited it by its own nonperformance. . . .

Woodrow Wilson, speech at Buffalo, New York, *Papers of Woodrow Wilson,* vol. 25, ed. Arthur S. Link (Princeton, N.J.: Princeton University Press, 1978), 72–85.

I want to speak upon this occasion, of course, on the interests of the workingman, of the wage earner, not because I regard the wage earners of this country as a special class, for they are not. After you have made a catalogue of the wage earners of this country, how many of us are left? The wage earners of this country, in the broad sense, constitute the country. And the most fatal thing that we can do in politics is to imagine that we belong to a special class, and that we have an interest which isn't the interest of the whole community. Half of the difficulties, half of the injustices of our politics have been due to the fact that men regarded themselves as having separate interests which they must serve even though other men were done a great disservice by their promoting them.

We are not afraid of those who pursue legitimate pursuits provided they link those pursuits in at every turn with the interest of the community as a whole; and no man can conduct a legitimate business, if he conducts it in the interest of a single class. I want, therefore, to look at the nation as a whole today. I would like always to look at it as a whole, not divide it up into sections and classes, but I want particularly to discuss with you today the things which interest the wage earner. That is merely looking at the country as a whole from one angle, from one point of view, to which for the time being we will confine ourselves. . . .

Very well then, what does this [Progressive party] platform propose to do? Break up the monopolies? Not at all. It proposes to legalize them. It says in effect: You can't break them up, the only thing you can do is to put them in charge of the federal government. It proposes that they shall be adopted and regulated. And that looks to me like a consummation of the partnership between monopoly and government. Because, when once the government regulates monopoly, then monopoly will have to see to it that it regulates the government. This is a [beautiful] circle of change.

We now complain that the men who control these monopolies control the government, and it is in turn proposed that the government should control them. I am perfectly willing to be controlled if it is I, myself, who control me. If this partnership can be continued, then this control can be manipulated and adjusted to its own pleasure. Therefore, I want to call your attention to this fact that these great combined industries have been more inimical to organized labor than any other class of employers in the United States. Is not that so?

These monopolies that the government, it is proposed, should adopt are the men who have made your independent action most difficult. They have made it most difficult that you should take care of yourselves; and let me tell you that the old adage that God takes care of those who take care of themselves is not gone out of date. No federal legislation can change that thing. The minute you are taken care of by the government you are wards, not independent men. And the minute they are legalized by the government, they are protégés and not monopolies. They are the guardians and you are the wards. Do you want to be taken care of by a combination of the government and the monopolies? [*A voice from the audience: "No."*] Because the working-men of this country are perfectly aware that they sell their commodity, that is to say labor, in a perfectly open market. There is free trade in labor in the United States. The laboring men of all the world are free to come and offer their labor here and you are similarly free to go and offer your labor in most parts of the world. And the world demand is what establishes for the most part the rate of wages, at the same time that these gentlemen who are paying the wages in a free-trade market are protected by an unfree market against the competition that would make them [bid] higher because [bid] in competition and not [bid] under protection. If I am obliged to refrain from going into a particular industry by reason of the combination that already exists in it, I can't become an employer of labor, and I can't compete with these gentle-men for the employment of labor. And the whole business of the level of wages is artificially and arbitrarily determined. . . .

What has created these monopolies? Unregulated competition. It has permitted these men to do anything that they chose to do to squeeze their rivals out and to crush their rivals to the earth. We know the processes by which they have done these things. We can prevent those processes by remedial legislation, and that remedial leg-islation will so restrict the wrong use of competition that the right use of competition will destroy monopoly. In other words, ours is a pro-gram of liberty and theirs is a program of regulation. Ours is a pro-gram by which we find we know the wrongs that have been committed and we can stop those wrongs. And we are not going to adopt into the governmental family the men who forward the wrongs and license them to do the whole business of the country. . . .

24

WOODROW WILSON

Speech at Sioux City, Iowa
September 17, 1912

Wilson delivered this speech approximately two weeks before requesting that Brandeis "set forth as explicitly as possible the actual measures by which competition can be effectively regulated." (See Document 20.) In the speech Wilson demonstrated a vague understanding of corporate growth and Brandeis's ideas, stating "I am for big business and I am against the trusts."

. . . A trust is an arrangement to get rid of competition and a big business is a business that has survived competition by conquering in the field of intelligence and economy. I am for big business and I am against the trusts. Any man that can survive by his brains, any man that can put the others out of business by making the thing cheaper to the consumer at the same time that he is increasing its intrinsic value and quality, I take off my hat to and I say, "You are the man who can build up the United States and I wish there were more of you."

But the third party says that trusts have come and they are inevitable; that is the only way of efficiency. I would say parenthetically that they don't know what they are talking about because the trusts are not efficient. If I had time for another speech I could prove that to you. They have passed the point of efficiency. Their object is not efficiency, though when they sell you their stock they say it is. Their object is monopoly, is the control of the market, is the shutting out by means fair or foul of competition in order that they may control the product.

Now, the third party says these things have come to stay. Mind you, these are artificially built-up things, these things that can't maintain themselves in the market without monopoly, have come to stay, and the only thing that the government can do, the only thing that the

Woodrow Wilson, speech at Sioux City, Iowa, in *A Crossroads of Freedom: The 1912 Campaign Speeches of Woodrow Wilson,* ed. John Wells Davidson (New Haven: Yale University Press, 1956), 157–65.

third party proposes should be done, is to set up a commission which is to regulate them. It accepts them. It says: "We will not undertake it, it were futile to undertake, to prevent monopoly in this country, but we will go into an arrangement by which we will make these monopolies kind to you. We will guarantee that they shall be pitiful. We guarantee that they shall pay the right wages. We guarantee that they shall do everything kind and public-spirited, which they have never heretofore shown the least inclination to do; and everything that we do for pure food, everything that we do for the rectification of things that have been done wrong, hereafter, shall be done through the trusts which we ourselves regulate."

Don't you realize that is a blind alley? You can't find your way to liberty that way. You can't find your way to pure food or anything else. I am merely using pure food as an illustration. You can't find your way to social reform through the forces which have made social reform necessary. Let them first set the government free and then we will follow them or any other honest men in setting up a schedule of social reform.

Now, there are things that have to be regulated, but they are not to be regulated through the trusts. They are to be regulated by those processes, now perfectly discoverable, by which monopoly can be prevented and broken up; because these monopolies that are to be made permanent if this program goes through, these monopolies are the very things that are limiting the field of enterprise, limiting the market for labor, determining the wages of labor, determining the distribution of products throughout the country. Take one instance—the twenty-four gentlemen who constitute the directors of the United States Steel Corporation act either as presidents or vice-presidents or members of the boards of directors of more than half the railways of the United States. Now, if you want to sell steel and ship steel and are in the board of directors of a railway that is carrying steel, what do you think is going to happen? Are you going to play into your own hand or aren't you? And since you are on the inside, do you think you are going to find out how to play into your own hand or are you not? I tell you, the tentacles of these things spread in every direction, and until we have broken their inside control, the government is helpless to assist the people to righteous processes of judgment and of law.

There are two instruments that the people use in government, two voices, for after all it is what is known, what is spoken, what is believed that moves great bodies of opinion in a free country like ours. What heartens me in recent years is to see how our political audiences have grown more and more serious; how they really want to hear something said; how they really want to get some argument that they can get their teeth in and not hear buncombe, not hear rhetoric. I dare say I could build up structures of rhetoric myself, but they are too thin. I don't want to climb on them, they are too insubstantial, and the American people isn't going to be fed any longer with words. . . .

Now these are the questions, and this is a cross section of the question of the day. What are we going to do with our government? First of all, determine what our government is. What are you going to do with a particular instrument? What is that instrument suited to do? You [have] first got to make sure of your instrument; then you can do what you wish to do with it.

For my part, I believe that we are upon the eve of recovering some of the most important prerogatives of the American people. You know that only a few years ago, for example, we were not interested in questions of the initiative and the referendum. I met a man the other day who thought the referendum was some kind of an animal because it had a Latin name, and there are people in this country, I think, who have never [had] it explained to them what the initiative and the referendum are. But we are interested in them now. Why? Because we have felt that in those many instances our governments didn't represent us, and we said: "We have got to have a key to the door of our own house. The initiative and the referendum are keys to our own premises. That is what they are. Now, if the people inside will run the business as we want it run, we will keep those latchkeys in our pockets. But if they don't, we will get them out and re-enter upon possession, and the government trying to act through the trusts will need to have the latchkey used on it very often." So that the whole impulse of American life is now an impulse of seeing things as they are. That is the reason that party lines are breaking—some party lines.

I don't notice any serious breaks in the Democratic line, but parties are getting a good deal mixed, not because we are getting mixed in our minds but because we are getting independent in our action; not because we are losing any reverence whatever for the great history of parties which have saved the nation in moments of emergencies and of crisis but because we have come upon a new kind of emergency and a new sort of crisis and are determined that we are going to have an instrument suitable to serve us now in the year 1912. . . .

25

WOODROW WILSON

Speech at Pueblo, Colorado
October 7, 1912

After receiving Brandeis's material, Wilson demonstrated a more detailed understanding of the anticorporate argument. Instead of equivocating between "big business" and "trusts" as he did in Document 24, Wilson focused on rolling back corporate growth as the key to democratic freedom. He stated, "unless we can set private monopoly aside, the enterprise of carrying the government back to the people is impossible."

The only principle involved in this campaign is: What are we going to do with our economic life? In order to do something new with it you have to have a new attitude with regard to tariff, and neither of these sections of the Republican party has a new attitude with regard to the tariff. In order to make any change in the life of the United States you have got to have a new attitude towards trusts and monopolies, and neither branch of the Republican party has changed its attitude towards monopoly. If you don't change the fundamental attitude, then you cannot go [on] the journey of liberty. If you don't face the sun, the sun will not shine in your eyes. You have got to face away from the ideals of monopoly or else you are not bound for the land of freedom.

I have had this image in my mind all morning that the humanistic, the humanitarian part of the third party's program is a sort of chorus which Mr. Roosevelt is trying to teach the trusts to sing because the fundamental part of that program is that the trusts shall be recognized as a permanent part of our economic order, and that the government shall try to make those trusts the ministers, the instruments, through which the life of this country shall be developed on its industrial side.

Woodrow Wilson, speech at Pueblo, Colorado, in *A Crossroads of Freedom: The 1912 Campaign Speeches of Woodrow Wilson*, ed. John Wells Davidson (New Haven: Yale University Press, 1956), 355–62.

Now, everything that touches our lives sooner or later goes back to the industries which sustain our lives. I have often reflected that there was a very human order in the petitions in our Lord's Prayer. For we pray first of all, "Give us this day our daily bread," knowing that it is useless to pray for spiritual graces on an empty stomach, and that, therefore, the physical part of our life—the industrial part of it, the amount of wages we get, the kind of clothes we wear, the kind of food we can afford to buy—is fundamental to everything else. . . .

We are going to decide on the fifth of November not whether we will overcome and govern them but whether we will attempt to overcome and govern them; for neither branch of the Republican party proposes to set private monopoly aside, and unless we can set private monopoly aside, the enterprise of carrying the government back to the people is impossible. The Democratic platform says that private monopoly is in every case indefensible and intolerable, and I subscribe literally to that statement. I shall stand in any position that I may occupy, shall stand with all the strength that is within me, against every form of monopoly and private control. And I call upon the people of this country to beware of making a choice which will perpetuate private control, and I call upon them particularly in the interest of those fine sentences of the chorus that Mr. Roosevelt is trying to teach the trusts to sing. I believe in that chorus—it stirs my blood.*
[But I do not believe it can be sung under such auspices.]

I believe that the time has come when the governments of this country, both state and national, have to set the stage—and set it very minutely and carefully—for the doing of justice to men in every relationship of life. It has been free and easy with us so far; it has been [go as you please; it has been] every man look out for himself; and we have assumed that in this year when every man is dealing, not with another man, in most cases, but with a body of men whom he has not seen, that the relationships between capital and labor are the same that they always were, and that the relationships of property are the same that they always were.

Let me call your attention to one process of monopoly in this country. Certain monopolies in this country have gained control of the raw material, chiefly in the mines, out of which a great body of manufactures is carried on, and they now discriminate in the sale of that

---

*Some cartoonists picked up on Wilson's statement and put his criticism in cartoon form. For an example, see Document 26.

raw material between those who are rivals of the monopoly and those who submit to the monopoly. And we have got to come to a time, ladies and gentlemen, when we shall say to every man who owns the essentials of life that he has got to part with those essentials by sale to every citizen of the United States upon the same terms, or else we shall tie up the resources of this country under private control in such fashion as will make our independent development absolutely impossible.

Then there is another way that monopoly acts. The monopoly that deals in the cruder products which are to be manufactured into the more elaborate manufactures will not sell those crude products except upon the terms of monopoly—that is to say, the people that deal with them will buy exclusively from them. And so again you have the lines of development tied up and the connections of development knotted and fastened so that you can't wrench them apart.

Not only so, but most of the big trusts in this country have been the professed, the avowed, the active opponents and enemies of organized labor. And they only have been the successful opponents of organized labor.

And why has labor organized? Simply because capital organized. And the law of this country does not yet recognize that labor has the same right to organize that capital has. Individuals cannot deal with an organization. Organizations must deal with organizations if there is to be any equality in the terms of dealing. And when I say that monopoly should be broken up in this country, I esteem myself a champion of the laborers of this country because I know that monopoly is stiffening and closing and commanding the market of labor, just as much as it is stiffening and closing the markets for the products which the monopolies produce. Everything is falling into the lines which these gentlemen plan, for if you reduce the number of competitors, you of course eliminate the competition; and there is no competition for labor after you have eliminated this its rival. And, therefore, the prices, wages, can be fixed by the same sort of monopolistic agreements by which the prices of production are fixed, and I don't find the prices of production bearing any particular relationship to the wages paid....

Evidence of what I am about to say comes to me by way of corroboration every day in forms that I cannot question. It is a very interesting circumstance that the [United States] Steel Corporation is behind the third-party program with regard to the regulation of the trusts.

Now, I don't say that in order to prejudice you, because I am not here to indict anybody. I am perfectly ready to admit that the officers of the United States Steel Corporation may think that is the best thing for the United States. That is not my point. My point is that these gentlemen have grown up in the atmosphere of the things they themselves have created, and that the law of the United States so far has attempted to destroy the things that they have created, and that they now want a government which will perpetuate the things they have created. You, therefore, have to choose now a government such as the United States Steel Corporation, that is to say, such as the men who promote trusts and monopolies think the United States ought to have, or a government such as we used to have before these gentlemen succeeded in setting up private monopoly. You can tell the character of a thing by the thought of the men who are behind it, not necessarily by the character of the men who are behind it. . . .

ST. LOUIS POST DISPATCH

The Biggest Monopolies
October 9, 1912

To highlight his critique of Roosevelt's New Nationalism, Wilson proclaimed that if he were a cartoonist he would "draw a picture of the biggest monopolies of the United States, drawn up in line and in front Mr. Roosevelt trying to lead them in a hallelujah chorus." Wilson's statement, and the numerous cartoons that followed it, suggested that Roosevelt would act to encourage corporate growth, not to control it. (For a similar comment from Wilson, see Document 24.)

St. Louis Post Dispatch, October 9, 1912, 12.

OSWALD GARRISON VILLARD

Diary

August 14, 1912

This excerpt comes from the diary of social reformer and publisher Oswald Garrison Villard. Throughout the campaign, Wilson stood opposed to a national women's suffrage amendment. Although Villard, who was one of the founders of the National Association for the Advancement of Colored People (NAACP), was "delighted" with Wilson's promises on racial issues, Wilson proved to be a great disappointment to many reformers. He appointed ardent segregationists to high cabinet positions and segregated federal government facilities.

I had a long and interesting interview with Woodrow Wilson yesterday. . . .

On the negro question, . . . I was quite delighted with his attitude. He said that, of course, he should be President of all the people, that he would appoint no man to office because he was colored, any more than he would appoint one because he was a Jew or a Catholic, but that he would appoint him on his merits. "The only place," he said, "where you and I will differ is as to where the entering wedge should be driven." He stated that he would not make an appointment like that of Crum at Charleston because he felt that it resulted in very great injury to the colored people and increased race antipathy, which, he said, we must try to avoid. . . . Again, I told him of the conditions of the colored people which prevented their being able to lift a voice in their own government, and of the 5000 colored children walking the streets of Atlanta without hope of an education, predestined to vice and crime and ignorance. I told him the Virginia Christian story, which also moved him not a little, and how they were killing that girl this week because being a child of a child race and compelled to live in the horrible slums, more or less of an outcast, she had had no chance to be anything else than what she was.*

*In 1912 Virginia Christian, a seventeen-year-old African American girl was executed, despite many public pleas for mercy, by the State of Virginia for killing her white employer.

Oswald Garrison Villard, excerpt from diary, in *Papers of Woodrow Wilson,* vol. 25, ed. Arthur S. Link (Princeton, N.J.: Princeton University Press, 1978), 24–26.

This made quite an impression upon him, and he told me with a great deal of feeling of the "worst phase" of his governorship; that the poor and victims of injustice find their way to him all the time and that he cannot help them because the Governor of New Jersey has no power in such matters. He said of course he would speak out against lynching, "every honest man must do so," but that he did not wish the colored people to get the impression that he could help them in that matter as President, as the President had no power. He has promised me a statement probably for the Crisis and the Evening Post, or if not, one to be spread broadcast to help me in writing a letter to the negro newspapers and otherwise helping his candidacy.

I then presented a letter to him from Mrs. Fitzgerald, written to me, begging a statement from him on the woman suffrage question saying that he was losing thousands of votes in Massachusetts because of Roosevelt's advocacy of suffrage. He said, — "I have no doubt it is true," and said that Roosevelt would gain an enormous advantage in the woman suffrage States, but that he was not like Roosevelt and could not change his opinion in order to get votes. He said, "I cannot do anything"; I said "You certainly cannot change now unless you are converted, without putting yourself in Roosevelt's class." He said that was it exactly.

28

NEW YORK TIMES

Maud Malone Halts Wilson

October 20, 1912

Wilson's stand against women's suffrage brought strong opposition. During the speech described in this article, suffrage activist Maud Malone interrupted Wilson's talk to point out the contradiction between his support for democratic action against trusts and his opposition to granting the vote to women.

"Maud Malone Halts Wilson," *New York Times,* October 20, 1918, 4.

Big Crowd Sees Militant Suffragist Dragged from Brooklyn Academy

Gov. Woodrow Wilson and Representative William Sulzer talked for the Democratic cause in the Brooklyn Academy of Music last night and discussed the same issues. The striking difference in their presence on the stage was that the speech of Gov. Wilson was cut in two in the middle by an interruption by Maud Malone, the militant suffragist. The interruption was so serious that it really caused an intermission of about five minutes in the set programme, and it only ceased when Miss Malone was dragged out of the building by two big policemen, hustled down a fire escape, and locked up in the Bergen Street Police Station on a charge of disorderly conduct. It was the first time that the question of woman's rights had been thrust directly in Gov. Wilson's face....

...Andrew McLean...presented Gov. Wilson, and the uproar when the Governor appeared before the footlights were hearty and sincere. He stood and smiled upon the commotion, and when it grew quiet he began to speak. He got to the point where the discussion of monopolies was taken up. He said:

"But just as long as there is some private influence at work to control the Government then the conscience of every public spirited man who loves America will be against the men who are trying to control the Government of the United States for that purpose. There is a bigger monopoly than any monopoly that is ordinarily mentioned on the stump."

This was the cue for Miss Malone. She rose in her seat in the first balcony, midway between the centre and the left aisle and cried out in a loud voice:

"How about votes for women?"

Everybody turned toward the voice, and a woman was seen standing erect, with her arms hanging stiff and straight at her sides. She wore a purple shirtwaist and jewels flashed from her neck. After the audience had looked at her there came a yell of "Put her out."

Gov. Wilson held up his hand and got as near the footlights as he could. He asked the people to wait for a minute, and the people waited for a few breathless seconds. Then the Governor looked up at Miss Malone, and in his softest voice asked:

"What is it, Madame?"

Miss Malone then cried out in a tone that was plainly heard all over the hall:

"Mr. Wilson, you just said you were trying to destroy a monopoly, and I ask you what about woman suffrage? The men have a monopoly."

There was a burst of laughter at this and it was a good thing, for it restored the big crowd to good humor. Gov. Wilson had stood with his hands clasped before him listening respectfully to Miss Malone. Then he answered her:

"Woman suffrage, madame, is not a question that is dealt with by the National Government at all. I am here only as the representative of the National party."

Cheers greeted this retort and then there were more yells of "Put her out." Gov. Wilson still kept on asking the crowd to be quiet and patient.

But Miss Malone was not afraid. She appeared to be perfectly calm and unmoved as she said:

"I am speaking to you as an American, Mr. Wilson." . . .

Gov. Wilson leaned as far over the stage as he could with safety and said:

"I hope you will not consider it a discourtesy if I decline to answer on this occasion."

There was another burst of applause at this, and when Miss Malone still held her place the temper of the crowd grew resentful and it yelled for her to take her seat. There were fiercer cries to put her out, and voices also called for the police.

A big voice asked her:

"Why don't you go to your own meeting?"

The disturbance was rapidly growing beyond control, and the Chairman rose and said:

"As Chairman of this meeting I must insist upon the lady taking her seat. That I insist upon as Chairman without any discourtesy to anybody. Gov. Wilson must not be interrupted any further."

But the yells continued, and an usher came over and took hold of Miss Malone's arm. She wrenched herself free and again stood rigid.

"The lady must take her seat," came from the chair.

A man yelled out for Miss Malone to go home and mind the babies. There was an outburst of laughter at this, and then came a chorus of yells to "put her out." Gov. Wilson kept moving about the stage and trying to get order. He begged the people to listen to him, and then he said:

"I am sure the lady will not insist when I positively decline to discuss the question now."

In a perfectly composed voice Miss Malone asked:

"Why do you decline?"

A citizen seized Miss Malone by the sleeve, but some men near her loudly protested at this and demanded that she be released. Judge Otto Kempner walked over to her and said:

"I am a Judge, and if you don't behave yourself I will have you placed under arrest."

But Miss Malone paid no attention. The crowd had lost all patience, and it yelled with delight when the big figure of Police Captain Bernard Hayes was seen marching down the aisle. Behind him came Lieut. John Walsh and Patrolman Dubois. There was no ceremony now. Miss Malone was seized in front and pushed from behind, and she went out of her seat in a big hurry. Once she stumbled and the police waited for her to recover her balance, when they gayly resumed the work of putting her out. The nearest exit was on the fire escape, and it was through this that Miss Malone was taken and hurried down stairs.

Then Gov. Wilson went on with his speech. . . .

29

CHICAGO DAILY TRIBUNE

The Time, the Place, and the Girl
June 25, 1912

This cartoon, drawn in the days before the Democratic National Convention, reveals three central themes of the 1912 election. First, to most observers, the election was the Democrats' to win after the split in the Republican party. Second, and more important, the caption on the laurel wreath, "Victory for Some Real Progressive," points to the central issue of 1912: the fight over control of progressive reform. And finally, Progressivism, a movement sometimes termed "municipal housekeeping," featured women in prominent positions— an idea reflected in both the caption of the cartoon and the depiction of "opportunity" as a female figure.

Chicago Daily Tribune, June 25, 1912, 1.

6

Neither a "Flubdub" nor Second Rate: William Howard Taft

30

WILLIAM HOWARD TAFT

Speech at Nashua, New Hampshire
March 19, 1912

In this speech, delivered after Roosevelt entered the race for the Republican presidential nomination, Taft expressed views that ran counter to popular ideology, defending the role of political parties and arguing against the widespread increase in popular power and direct democracy. His notion of government by a "representative part of the people" contrasted sharply with that offered by Roosevelt and La Follette.

Mr. Chairman, Ladies and Gentlemen:
... We are a government of the people, but when we say that we have not by any means solved the question. Popular government is one of the most difficult kinds of government to carry on, because in some way or other we have to mass the opinions of individuals and apply that composite opinion to the operations of government. ...

... We recognize—all of us—that the judgment of the people is not as good at a single jump or on a single expression as it is after some time is taken for deliberation and time is taken for ascertaining facts. After that comes, after we have the machinery which permits deliberation and a knowledge of the facts, then we know and feel that

William Howard Taft, speech at Nashua, New Hampshire, *William Howard Taft Papers* (microfilm edition), series 9A, reel 570.

the best expression, that the best government is found in popular government thus arranged. So when we begin to found popular government we must establish rules—fundamental rules—for the structure, and the means by which this popular will is to be interpreted. We all have recognized—at least our ancestors did—that the only possible way by which that can be safe and secure the rights of the individuals and the rights of the minority and the rights of the non-voting majority, is to have a constitution which shall limit the power of the people in one election to do what they would do. In other words, if the people by one election could destroy our present government and take up some other, then we should be subject to momentary passion, one that we all recognize would be dangerous to the body politic.

Now let us see how we do now. We have a majority of the adult males.—you have in New Hampshire—at least I believe you have not yet extended suffrage to the women . . . who do the voting. They represent not more than one-fourth of all your people. Now they act in a sort of representative capacity for everybody else; but the object of government is for the benefit of every individual, whether it be the baby at the breast, or the old man tottering to the grave, or the woman or the girl, or the old woman—all of them are citizens, and all of them are entitled to the same rights—inalienable rights—as they are called, secured in the constitution. Under those conditions, are you going to arrange it so that a single vote upon the question of constitutional interpretation you are going to let that one-fourth take away the right that secures to you liberty and enables you by the writ of habeas corpus to go before a court and question whether your detention is lawful or not? Are you going to let that majority say by a momentary vote whether your property shall be taken away from you without due compensation? I do not think so, and I think you may reach that conclusion without in any way reflecting on the whole people.

This is a government of the whole people, for the whole people, by a representative part of the people, and in order to secure the rights of the minority and of the individual which are secured in the bill of rights in the constitution, you have to have a constitution and a bill of rights that limits the action of the voting majority. Now in order that you shall do so you have to have somebody to say when that majority of voters steps over the line of rights of the non-voting majority of women and children and others who don't vote, or of the voting minority that do vote, or of the individual, and who is that? Why that is the judiciary. They are the ones who are to say and rule whether the majority is keeping within the limits of that constitution and is preserving those inalienable rights to the individual for which government ultimately is established. . . . I ask you what you think of a system that when the Judge shall say no to the majority of voters, "No you can not do this, this is a violation of the constitution, you are usurping the powers that you have under it," leaves to this majority of voters to say whether that Judge shall continue on the Bench? Is not that giving to a defeated party in the controversy an opportunity to call the Judge down and to put in another Judge who will decide as that majority desires? The very keystone of our constitutional government, the very keystone of our popular government, the very keystone of securing the inalienable rights of life, liberty and property, is the independence of the judiciary.

But there is another form that is proposed. It is said that we ought to recall decisions, that is when there is a constitutional question up, and this voting majority—one-fourth of the people—does not like the decision of the Supreme court, that then it may recall that decision by a simple majority vote. Suppose you had an issue of this sort with some very unpopular people who had been lawless and had murdered people and that sort of thing were provided for in a law which really took away their right of liberty and deprived them of the writ of *habeas corpus,* that the popular feeling was so bitter against them that when the court decided that they had that right, the majority of the voting people said, "No, we will reverse that decision—they are not entitled to any rights anyhow—they are outlaws, and so we will reverse that decision," and they vote to reverse that decision and the decision is reversed, and those men are deprived of the writ of habeas corpus and the right to personal liberty.* Then after a while another law is passed doing the same thing with respect to somebody else or some class of people that are much more popular. What is the vote going to be then? I ask you whether in popular elections the vote in such cases is not likely to turn on what is actually done by the law rather than whether it conflicts with the constitution or not, so that we should have in one case and with respect to one class of individuals a vote sustaining the validity of such a law, and with respect to another class of people more popular, a vote overruling it and holding it to be unconstitutional. You would have a government of special instances. . . .

It is said I am distrusting the people in saying so, that the people who make the constitution ought to be able to interpret it. In the first

---

*A writ of habeas corpus requires that a person who is arrested be swiftly brought before a judge so that the charges against him or her can be investigated and ruled upon. This right is guaranteed in Article I, Section 9 of the United States Constitution.

place, that is not true. A constitution is a declaration of general principles. The question whether a particular law comes within the constitution or violates it is frequently a question very complex in working out, and it needs jurists, it needs eminent judges to say so, and I dare say so of the people and you dare say so of the people, because you know it. Now why should that be called a reflection on the people, and why should that be called a distrust of the people. . . .

In this representative government the government of the people is by selecting those to represent the people who are best fitted to do the work that the people desire to be done, and it is no reflection on the people to say so. Our people have a higher degree of intelligence than any people in the world, but that is not to say that everyone of them can play on the violin. That is not to say that everyone is fitted to do the professional work that may have to be done in behalf of the people. The man who tells the truth to the people is the real friend of the people, and not the one who is constantly flattering them into the belief that they are capable of something that they are not capable of. The American people are great. Why? They have established a government that has been enduring? Why. Because they have had the common sense in their constitution and in their laws and in their structure of government to face the fact that they can not trust themselves under all circumstances and that they are going to put into that fundamental law the restrictions by which they shall secure from themselves and their representatives that deliberation and that study and that knowledge of the facts that will enable them to act wisely when they do act. . . .

Government is for the purpose of securing the greatest good to the greatest number and also the greatest happiness and an opportunity for the pursuit of happiness to every individual. What we are striving for is not equality of condition. It is the socialists that want to force that division of property that they think it is possible to maintain and still have a motive for effort in the community. We disagree with them. We believe that if you take away the right of property you can not substitute anything to take its place. We do not believe that you can substitute anything for private property that will elevate human nature to what it is. Therefore I believe in the right of property, but I also believe that it is the business of the Government in so far as it may, by removing obstructions and by legislative aid, where it is possible, to create an equality of opportunity so that everybody striving under the motive of private property and the freedom of liberty that is given in this country may have nearly as equal an opportunity to raise himself from a humble position to one high and comfortable, and that everyone having that opportunity may feel that he has it and go to work and restrain himself and devote his attention and his industry with the thought that there is nothing between his being a messenger boy and accomplishing the supposed happiness of becoming President of the United States.

31

WILLIAM HOWARD TAFT

Speech at the American Academy of Political and Social Science
March 30, 1912

This speech provided Taft's clearest statement on economic and corporate policy. Taft emphasized his support for the Sherman Act as existing law, arguing that recent court action proved the effectiveness of the policies of his administration.

Ladies and Gentlemen:
I understand generally that this is a discussion of the question of the legality and illegality of industrial combinations, and that it involves incidentally the question of the enforcement of the anti-trust law of the United States, and the anti-trust laws of the States. I have been engaged for twenty years in construing the anti-trust law of the United States, and I think I know what it means. I have been told that the business people of the community do not know. I have observed that those who are not in the particular industrial combination that violates the law, but who are in competition with it, understand exactly the application of the law to that industrial combination.

William Howard Taft, speech at the American Academy of Political and Social Science, *William Howard Taft Papers* (microfilm edition), series 9A, reel 570.

I believe that the law has been explained by the Supreme Court of the United States in such a way that most business men can understand it, if they desire to. I recognize the fact that it renders unlawful, combinations and agreements which before its passage were regarded as proper avenues of business enterprise, and that it is very difficult to secure conviction of any person for violation of that law by a jury when it is supposed that the conviction is going to send men to prison. I am in favor of the enforcement of the law, but I believe in enforcing it in the way which is best adapted to secure compliance with it. I think it ought to be done by equitable proceedings directed toward the transaction itself, until the public and the business men are educated up to understanding what it is. I think that we must retain the law, my friends. I don't think we can permit the gathering together of these great industrial combinations that are illegal, merely by a desire to secure a reduction in the cost of production. Up to a certain point, it is true that the accumulation of plant will reduce the cost of production, but beyond that when you lose the benefit of the personal equation of the manager, and when you enlarge the plant so that it covers the country, you increase the expense of the production rather than reduce it; and the accumulation after that, therefore, is not for the purpose of reducing the cost of production, but it is for the purpose of controlling the business and controlling prices.

Now I am not in favor of persecution or running amuck among the businesses of the country. That is not the policy of the Government, but it is to treat that law as any other law, and enforce it so long as from legitimate sources of our information we find violations of it, and so long as the law is on the statute book we propose to continue that policy; but we are not engaged in trying to strike down the business of this country. Where combinations of this sort show themselves willing to come within the law, the Attorney-General is only too willing to enter a decree by consent, if need be, enforcing the law, and dividing up the great combinations into lesser combinations. The operation of the Tobacco Company and the Standard Oil decrees are pointed to as an indication that they are ineffective.* Nobody can say that. They are great combina-

---

*In 1911, using the Sherman Antitrust Act, the U.S. Supreme Court delcared that Standard Oil and the American Tobacco Company should be dissolved. However, the dissolution took a great deal of time and failed to limit Standard Oil and American Tobacco's economic power. Rather than serving as victories for antitrust prosecutions, these decisions were seen as an example of the weakness of the Sherman Act and the failure of antitrust prosecutions as a national policy.

tions, the division of which and the effect of the division of which you can not understand until two or three years have passed. The increase in the value of the stock is doubtless due to the competition—in the desire to secure control of one company or the other, and until two or three years have passed, you can not speak of the effectiveness of the decrees of the Supreme Court. My own judgment is that a decree entered as this is, with a continuing injunction, is the most effective method of enforcing the competition or the motive for competition that is needed to break up the control of prices. It is a serious problem, and I don't speak with confidence or certainty. I only speak with the judgment that I have formed from a study of the law and an observation of its effect that a judicial experience of eight or ten years and an executive experience of three or four have given me. We can not afford to be under the absolute control of a few men in business, any more than we can in any other branch of life, and we must take such steps as are necessary to protect ourselves against control. . . .

Now, you remember in 1904 and 1908—I remember because I was in the campaign in those years—that we were calling out, and both sides were calling out, and there was a terrific noise, about the enforcement of the anti-trust law, and everybody that was said to be progressive was bloody about the enforcement of that law. Well, I got a lawyer who I thought knew how to organize a business office, and made him Attorney-General, and he got lawyers about him who were organized for the purpose of carrying on litigation in courts, and not for the purpose of running headlines in newspapers. We went ahead and began to enforce the anti-trust law against every combination that was brought properly to our attention. It was not very long before I met those same progressive gentlemen who were engaged in demanding the enforcement of the anti-trust law coming the other way and saying, "Here, you are interfering with business, you have no thought to the benefit of the public." Well, it just took my breath away. Nothing had been done with the law—it still remained on the statute book. It was there for enforcement under the oath which I had taken as President of the United States, and yet I was greeted from every part of the country with the statement, "You are destroying business." I was merely trying to carry out the promise I made in the last campaign, and the oath I had taken. The operation was misunderstood. It was supposed to be very much more destructive than it really was. Business men who never had violated the law were not quite certain whether they had or not, and they became frightened, and there was a kind of panic, and I found myself in that situation which had I not thought it comic I would regard as very serious. We can supplement this statute. We can supplement it by an incorporation act that shall bring close supervision to these great industrial enterprises that shall provide for the punishment of their officers when the law is violated, just as the officers of the national banks are punished, so that stockholders if they are not themselves guilty, need not be made to suffer. We can make a law which shall give to legitimate business that shall come within the supervision of the United States Government, that protection that will make all business possible and easy and legitimate, and I hope will secure the prosperity that legitimate business is entitled to. Now I have not had the benefit of what has gone before, and if I have said anything that was an absolute contradiction of what anybody else said, I apologize to him, but I don't take back the proposition.

32

WILLIAM HOWARD TAFT

Letters to Horace D. Taft and Charles F. Brooker
March 1, 1912, and March 5, 1912

Nothing caused greater concern among conservative Republicans than Roosevelt's proposal to subject judicial decisions to popular votes. (See Document 4.) In the letter to his brother, Taft rallied around conservatism, claiming that the most aggressive aspects of Roosevelt's speech (especially the proposal to recall judicial decisions) would work against Roosevelt. Although he denied mistrusting voters, Taft's reference to "the ignorant and the lower class voter" suggests that some of the concern over his attitude toward democracy was justified.

In the second letter, written to a friend and adviser, Taft developed the theme he first explored in the letter to his brother. Casting himself as the defender of judicial power and the Constitution, Taft was focused on winning the Republican nomination in order to keep the party from being radicalized by Roosevelt. Taft believed that even if he lost, maintaining the Republican party as the party of constitutional conservatism was the main issue of 1912.

William Howard Taft, letters, *William Howard Taft Papers* (microfilm edition), series 8, reel 510.

MARCH 1, 1912

My dear Horace:

I have yours of February 29th. The effect of Roosevelt's announcement and his Columbus speech has been sharply to call the attention of business men to the crisis that now impends. If he defeats me it means a campaign in which there will be a race of extreme radicalism by both candidates, and the chance of the conservatives to rally 'round any one who will defend the policies that they would naturally uphold will have disappeared. . . .

In every place where there are conservative business men and substantial property interests of any large size—and smaller ones too—there has been a revolution of feeling because of Roosevelt's Columbus speech and his announcement. [See Document 4.] The leaven is working in Ohio. I saw a man from Cleveland this morning, and he said that he did not find any one in Cleveland that was not against Roosevelt. Myron Herrick has been with me and he says the same thing. Of course, this doesn't refer to the ignorant and the lower class voter, but it sharpens the interest of the intelligent and the business community in the matter, much to my benefit. Ohio doesn't vote until the 21st of May so that there is time to remedy the unfavorable condition that undoubtedly has been there.*

In Indiana the fight is on, but the machine is a very perfect one, and I have every confidence in carrying the majority of the delegation. . . .

In Michigan, under the convention system I shall have at least one-half of the delegation—perhaps more. Indeed, I got two delegates instructed for me yesterday. But the lunatic Governor out there has called a special meeting of the legislature to provide for a Presidential primary.† The constitution prevents the immediate operation of any law except it be an appropriation or a law for the public health and public safety, and then only by two-thirds vote of each House. Plainly a law for a Presidential primary is not a law for the legislature to make immediately applicable. But this doesn't phase the Governor, who writes a message asking for the passage of such a law and the passage of a resolution making it immediately applicable, saying that while corporation lawyers and lawyers against the public interest would probably hold it unconstitutional, simple minded lawyers would hold the other way; and it must be constitutional because it is right, and whatever is right is constitutional.

---

*Taft was wrong. In the Ohio presidential primary Roosevelt defeated Taft with a strong plurality of the vote.

†Taft was referring to Governor Chase Osborn of Michigan, one of the governors who called for Roosevelt to enter the campaign. (See Document 3.)

That is the principle that actuates the whole Roosevelt crowd in reference to constitutional limitations. I have information that in the Senate there will probably be men enough with courage to recognize what a constitutional limitation is and to oppose it. In any event, I think the courts will probably throw out the law, so that we shall have the election of delegates by convention in Michigan.

The noise of the Roosevelt boom continues, and, while I hear that a good many who are the noisiest are not at all confident and, indeed, are rather disposed to give up the fight as hopeless, still I think it is serious enough to require every effort on my part. . . .

Affectionately,
Wm. H. Taft

March 5, 1912

CONFIDENTIAL

My dear Charlie:
I have your kind letter of March 4th and am glad to read what you write. The fight is going to be a hard one, but I think we are coming out ahead. The truth is that the crisis is on now from this time until the Convention—the real crisis for conservative men. If Colonel Roosevelt is nominated we shall have at the head of the Republican ticket an ultra-radical. This will lead the Democrats to nominate a radical as well, and the campaign will be a chase to see which can put his flag on the most extreme battlement of radicalism. It will disrupt the Republican party and there is no knowing when it will get together again for the purpose of reasserting its proper position in this government, which is that of progressive conservatism. I think, in spite of what Colonel Roosevelt and his supporters think and say, that before the people I shall be a stronger candidate than he; but, after all, that is not now the question. I am not quite sure which would be the more disastrous, in case of his nomination,—the election of a Democrat or of a Republican. On the other hand, if I were nominated, even though I were to go down to defeat, I should be on a conservative platform and should rally the conservative forces of this country and keep them in a nucleus of party strength, so that after four years the party could gather itself together and probably reestablish itself in control.

The campaign is a very hard and sad one for me. Considering my close relations with Colonel Roosevelt, my admiration for him as a man, my gratitude to him as one who made me President, and my appreciation of him as a chief with whom every relation was most delightful, it is hard for me now to be in opposition to him and feel that he is in bitter opposition to me. I do not mean to lend myself, in any way, to a personal controversy with him, but of course it will be impossible to keep our respective followers from using language that will irritate and embitter. . . .

As ever,
Sincerely yours

33

WILLIAM HOWARD TAFT

Speech at Elkton, Maryland
May 4, 1912

In speeches such as this one, Taft continued the critique of Roosevelt that he put forth in his letters. Taft appealed to conservatives worried by Roosevelt, casting himself as the defender of the Constitution and the separation of powers. Taft also used his defense of the Constitution to reargue that he was not antidemocratic, but instead the protector of constitutional liberty.

My friends of Elkton, Ladies and Gentlemen, My Fellow Citizens:
. . . I think we ought to thank God that we are Americans, that we have had a constitution for 125 years that was drawn by patriots for the purpose of maintaining and making permanent popular government, and that that constitution has served us well. What is it we have had for the last 125 years? Has it been anything but a rule of the people? What was it in Abraham Lincoln's time? Was it anything but a rule by the people? What was it in William McKinley's time? Was it anything but a rule of the people? What was it in Theodore Roosevelt's time? Was it anything but a rule of the people? But now in William Howard Taft's

William Howard Taft, speech at Elkton, Maryland, *William Howard Taft Papers* (microfilm edition), series 9A, reel 570.

time it has become a rule not by the people but by the bosses. Now my friends don't you think there is a good deal of fuss made for the purpose of arousing discontent with a condition of happiness that ought to exist among a people that has such a government as we have and such a constitution as we have that protects the rights of the humbled individual? . . . I agree that there are a great many abuses in our government, abuses that we are trying to remedy, but we have a constitution that makes this a popular government, and every time the people desire to rise and wipe out abuses they do it, and we are not a downtrodden people and we do not have to make an issue every time. . . .

Now my friends I would not be out here arguing this question if it concerned my personal ambition only and my personal reputation. I might get along without the office. I can trust to the future to wipe out the effect of these charges and let the future develop whether they are true or not, but I deem under the present circumstances that I [represent] a cause and that cause is the cause of constitutional government. It is the question whether we are going to destroy the independence of the judiciary, whether we are going to take away from our courts the power to interpret the constitution and turn it over to a single vote at a single election. Now I submit to you you would not like to have your rights and guaranties in the constitution submitted to a vote that may be determined one way or the other according as it is a democratic or republican year. You want that thing the constitution has fixed by the people through a constitutional convention after full deliberation, not with reference to a particular issue, but with reference to the future when general principles ought to prevail and do prevail. You don't want it determined as to a particular issue by a particular vote. You have men in your courts who interpret the constitution. What is the new doctrine? It is that if that interpretation is not liked, you will then submit it to the vote of the people to determine whether the lawyers whom you have put on the bench have correctly interpreted the constitution. As I say, if it is a democratic year it will go democratic way, and a Republican year it will go that way. Are you willing, do you wish to place the guaranties of your life, liberty and property that are implanted in the constitution to such a method of determining whether you shall have the writ of habeas corpus and those other rights that are secured to you by the fundamental law? It is a destruction of constitutional government, I say to you my friends with the dark-colored skins. It is true that Mr. Roosevelt says this is limited to state constitutions, but if you apply it to state constitutions, as they have already proposed it in Pennsylvania, what logical difference is there between that and applying it to the federal constitution? And then you have what? Whenever the people don't like a particular decision of the Supreme Court, then it is to be submitted to the people to overrule that and make an exception to the constitution with respect to a particular law. Now if the law is popular, then it will pass, and the constitution will be sustained as to that law. If it is not popular then it wont. And so you will have a construction of the constitution one way for this law, and another way for that law, and that is the kind of construction of the constitution you will have under this most remarkable suggestion of reform, and where will our colored friends be with the 14th and 15th amendments, and those things that they rely upon to secure them what the war brought about. . . .

Now it is said I am not a friend of the people because I distrust them. Any man who says that I distrust the people is inaccurate. It is said I distrust the people because I took the definition of the people that Lincoln gave and construed it and explained it. Lincoln referred to our government at Gettysburg as a government of the people, for the people and by the people. I went through that and attempted to show what he meant by it. It is a government of the people because it belongs to all the people—men, women and children. It is a government for the people because it is a government which protects the rights of every person within its jurisdiction, man, woman and child. The tottering old woman, the adult male, the youth, the babe at the breast, everyone is a citizen of the United States and entitled under that constitution to the right of life, liberty, property and the pursuit of happiness. Our Anglo Saxon ancestors did not allow themselves to be content with mere general declarations, but they provided the machinery right in the constitution by which liberty could be asserted. And so it is with the right of property and the pursuit of happiness. Now therefore it is a government for all the people. Then when you come to the question of government by the people you have to modify your definition if you would be exact. Who is it that carries on this government? Is it these children? Is it these ladies before us? You know and I know it is not. It is the adult males who cast the votes under your constitution. It is the majority of the voting population that is less than one-fourth of the entire population. Therefore a correct definition is to say it is a government by a representative part of the people. I pointed that out for the purpose of showing the necessity of having a constitution which should restrict the majority of the voters in what they did to the non-voters, and in what they did to the minority. Now what did Mr. Roosevelt do with that statement. He said, "By a representative part of the people," that means a government by the few, that means a government by an oligarchy, that means a government by an aristocracy, that means a government by bosses." Now my friends it is that kind of misrepresentation, it is that kind of misleading of the public that would put me on the side of the boss as an aristocrat, as an oligarch against the people that has led me to come out and bring the office of President. . . .

. . . What I attempted to do in my administration was carry out Mr. Roosevelt's policies, and one of those policies I thought to be the prosecution of the trusts under the anti-trust law, and so I gave orders to the Attorney-General to prosecute every trust that he found violating the law, and the only difference between me and Mr. Roosevelt is that I prosecuted the Steel Trust and the Harvester Trust, and he did not.[*] Now I am not making any charges against him, because he did not. He changed his mind about the operation of the anti-trust law, and he thinks now that its operation is not good, and he criticizes me because I prosecuted the Standard Oil Company and the Tobacco Company through to the Supreme Court and got decrees there.[†] . . . Any man who knows anything about it knows that my administration has prosecuted everything; every violation of law that has been properly brought to the attention of the Attorney-General. We are said to be under the influence of the railroads. Did not we stop the raising of rates by injunction suit in Missouri until the law now passed will prevent the railroads from raising rates until they can be examined by the Interstate Commerce commission, and have we not prosecuted every trust the evidence of whose violation has been brought to us. I am not claiming particular credit on that account. I was born and brought up a lawyer and I was on the bench for eight years. I am in favor of the enforcement of law, and while it is on the statute book and while I have control of power, I am going to prosecute it. . . .

---

[*] For Taft's view on the division, see Document 31.
[†] For Roosevelt's view, see Document 7.

CLEVELAND PRESS

He Eats 'Em Up—and Grows!

September 19, 1910

This cartoon was published in the wake of a number of victories by anti-Taft, insurgent candidates. It reflected the popular sense that the new reform-minded politicians were the rising generation in the Republican party, and that Taft and the conservatives with whom he had aligned himself would soon be pushed to the margins.

Cleveland Press, September 19, 1910, 8.

ST. LOUIS POST DISPATCH

The Presidency

September 29, 1912

By the time the election rolled around, many Americans, like this cartoonist, believed that Taft was simply no match for the job. The idea that Taft was too small for the great job of president is ironic because Taft was notoriously overweight, weighing more than three hundred pounds.

St. Louis Post Dispatch, September 29, 1912, 7.

CHICAGO DAILY NEWS

Progressive: The Popular Label

October 6, 1912

There's likely to be a big run on the popular label.

By election day, so many candidates were claiming to be the "true" Progressive that one cartoonist depicted all of the candidates (except Roosevelt) scrambling to fit themselves into the latest fad.

Reprinted in the *St. Louis Post Dispatch,* October 6, 1912, 3.

7

Socialism as Progressivism:
Eugene V. Debs

37

EUGENE V. DEBS

Socialism Gives Only Cure for Trust Evils
November 25, 1911

*In this 1911 article, Debs made two notable claims that became the
focus of his campaign. First, he argued that the Sherman Act was inade-
quate (in his words it was a "puerile and silly" piece of legislation) for
dealing with America's economic problems. As he stated, trust development was "the logical result of industrial evolution." Because corporate
growth was a natural development, Debs argued that "no intelligent
observer . . . believes the trust can be forced back into its constituent and
competing elements."*

*Debs's second point was a broader one. In arguing that the choice
between capitalism and socialism was a choice between industrial despotism and industrial democracy, he made socialism the equivalent of
democracy.*

TERRE HAUTE, IND., NOV. 23. — [SPECIAL.]
It is generally conceded that the trust is the logical result of industrial
evolution. This was the Socialist contention from the beginning, but it

Eugene V. Debs, "Holds Socialism Gives Only Cure for Trust Evils," *Chicago Tribune,*
November 25, 1911, in *Papers of Eugene V. Debs* (microfilm edition), reel 17.

met with strenuous denial until the acceptance of that view was finally compelled by the stern logic of events.

No student of economics and no intelligent observer of events believes the trust can be forced back into its constituent and competing elements to satisfy the cry of a defeated and doomed middle class. Only the academic charlatan and political demagogue, seeking to promote their own selfish ends yield to the clamor of the small interests that the trust be "smashed" and that we return to "the good old days of competition." . . .

Time was when competition in industry was constructive in its effect upon those engaged in it; now it is destructive, and every wise capitalist knows it and seeks escape from competition in the shelter and security of combination and coöperation.

Industrial Combination Certain

Industrial competition is as certain to culminate in industrial combination as that the millions of tributaries in the Mississippi valley are certain to unite in the Mississippi river.

To deal intelligently with the trust we must know, first of all, that the trust is simply the twentieth century tool of production, distribution, and exchange, and from the Socialist point of view there is but one question in reference to the trust that confronts the people, and that is shall the trust be privately owned by a relatively few and operated for their fabulous enrichment, or shall it be owned by the people in their collective, organized, and enlightened capacity and operated for the benefit of all?

And this is the choice between industrial despotism and industrial democracy, that is to say, between capitalism and socialism. . . .

. . . The Sherman anti-trust law was enacted by congress in 1890. It is no doubt true that a large share of good faith entered into that measure on the part of those who supported it but a more puerile, silly piece of legislation was never enacted. There is the same political wisdom and constructive statesmanship in that measure that there was in the pope's bull against the comet.

The Sherman anti-trust law was the first attempt to suspend by legislative enactment the laws underlying our industrial and social development. This measure would have applied with equal force to gravitation or the ebb and flow of the tides.

What combination has ever been restrained under the operation, or more properly, inoperation, of this so-called law? . . .

Quotes Talk by Roosevelt

From the Socialist viewpoint, therefore, the prosecution of the trusts is pure political buncombe, and this fact, so flagrantly in evidence to the thinking mind and discerning eye, would be apparent to all if so many of the people were not still in their mental childhood.

But the truth is slowly dawning upon the public, forced upon them by the logic of the conditions which surround them and which are becoming more and more intolerable as the trusts increase in power and tighten their strangle-hold upon the people.

And as the people awaken so do their leaders begin to see that light. Successful leaders are wise enough to follow the people. For instance, the following paragraph is to the point:

"Ultimately I believe that this control of corporations should undoubtedly, directly or indirectly, extend to dealing with all questions connected with their treatment of their employe[e]s, including the wages, the hours of labor, and the like."

Roosevelt Changes with Time

And what Socialist made himself ridiculous by such a foolish utterance? No Socialist at all; only a paragraph from his latest article on the trusts by Theodore Roosevelt. Five years ago, or when he was still in office and had the power, he would not have dared to make that statement. But he finds it politically safe and expedient to make it now. . . .

President Roosevelt, who is popularly supposed to be hostile to the trusts, is in truth their best friend. He would have the government, the capitalist government, of course, practically operate the trusts and turn the profits over to their idle owners. This would mean release from responsibility and immunity of prosecution for the trust owners, while at the same time the government would have to serve as strike-breaker for the trust owners, and the armed forces of the government would be employed to keep the working class in subjection.

Movement Cannot Be Fettered

If this were possible it would mark the half way ground between industrial despotism and industrial democracy. But it is not possible, at least only temporarily, long enough to demonstrate its failure. The expanding industrial forces now transforming society, realigning political parties and reshaping the government itself cannot be fettered in any such artificial arrangement as Mr. Roosevelt proposes. These forces with the rising and awakening working class in alliance with them will sweep all such barriers from the track of evolution until finally they can find full expression in industrial freedom and social democracy. . . .

One thing is certain and that is that the trust question will never be settled upon the basis of the exploitation of the working class. The trust question is above all else a working class question and only an enlightened working class can finally settle it.

Every conceivable attempt will be made to control and regulate the trusts and all will prove futile in the end; and yet all these are necessary to open the eyes of the people to what the trust actually is and to teach them how to deal with it intelligently so as to convert it from a menace into a blessing to society.

The trust is monumental of the fact that competition has run its course in our industrial life and that coöperation has taken its place as the basis of a more perfectly organized society, a higher social order, and a more advanced civilization. . . .

The millions of workers of all kinds who are employed in these trusts and who alone are necessary to their operation are organizing industrially and politically to take possession of them in the name of the people — socialize them, in a word — so that all may have the benefit of these modern social agencies of wealth production.

Everything about a trust has been socially produced and everything about it is socially used and the character of the trust marks it for social ownership.

We cannot go backward if we would; we are pushed onward by the forces that move society even in spite of ourselves.

As the trusts grow more and more powerful and the puny attempts to shackel them become more and more futile, the only alternative left will be to socialize them, have them owned by the people, and then, and not until then, can they be successfully controlled and regulated by government. . . .

38

APPEAL TO REASON

A Study of Competition

May 28, 1910

This article appeared in Appeal to Reason *three months before Roosevelt delivered his "New Nationalism" speech. (See Document 1.) Although Roosevelt and the Socialists offered very different programs, there was a striking parallel between Roosevelt's belief that corporate development was inevitable and the Socialist argument that "the trusts and monopolies of today are the natural development of industry."*

... The trusts and monopolies of today are the natural development of industry, and they are going to continue this development until the pressure becomes so severe that a change will be made necessary. Unless intelligence [and] understanding is used, that something will be very terrible, for in this age of schools and traditions of liberty, the many are not going to quietly sink into a modern serfdom as galling as was that of a thousand years ago. The danger lies not in the natural law of evolution, but in not understanding how to get the benefit of that law for all. ...

We are now at the threshold of a new order. Individual competition having run its course has now become monopoly, whether men wish it or not. The evidences of the new order are coming to light in every paper and magazine and book. The efforts to control the trusts and monopolies are the dim vision of the many that something is wrong and must be changed. This vision will become clearer and clearer, just as was the grasp of the individual competitive idea as the world emerged out of feudalism. The demand for municipal ownership of public utilities, the complaints and protests against court decisions favorable to the masters of industries, the many and increasing fraternal organizations and political demands; the insurgency of a few

---

"A Study of Competition," *Appeal to Reason,* 756, May 28, 1910, 2.

republicans, the efforts to get radical laws as relates to the owners of monopolies—all these are straws that presage the coming storm, or popular disapproval of the conditions that have grown out of the old system. . . .

We are to have greater and greater industries. Monopoly is certain and sure. It is merely a question of whether we will be collectively owned monopolies, for the good of the race, or whether they will be privately owned for the power, pleasure and glory of the Morgans, Rockefellers, Guggenheims and Carnegies. You have a choice between these two ways, but you have no other choice. One or the other it is certain to be.

One way is Socialism, for the good of all. The other is the belief in private capital, for the benefit of a few and the degradation and poverty of the many. . . .

39

EUGENE V. DEBS

Acceptance Speech

Undated

In accepting the presidential nomination for the Socialist party, Debs made the case for socialism in fairly traditional terms; however, his criticism of the Progressive party as the party of "progressive capitalism" pointed out the marked similarities among the Democrats, Republicans, and Progressives, despite the heated personal disagreements among the three candidates.

Speech of Acceptance

The Socialist Party is fundamentally different from all other parties. It came in the process of evolution and grows with the growth of the

Eugene V. Debs, *Writings and Speeches of Eugene V. Debs* (New York: Hermitage Press, 1948), 361–65.

forces which created it. Its spirit is militant and its aim revolutionary. It expresses in political terms the aspiration of the working class to freedom and to a larger and fuller life than they have yet known. . . .

The workers in the mills and factories, in the mines and on the farms and railways never had a party of their own until the Socialist Party was organized. They divided their votes between the parties of their masters. They did not realize that they were using their ballots to forge their own fetters.

But the awakening came. It was bound to come. Class rule became more and more oppressive and wage slavery more and more galling. The eyes of the workers began to open. They began to see the cause of the misery they had dumbly suffered so many years. It dawned upon them that society was divided into two classes—capitalists and workers, exploiters and producers; that the capitalists, while comparatively few, owned the nation and controlled the government; that the courts and the soldiers were at their command, and that the workers, while in a great majority, were in slavish subjection. . . .

The very suffering they were forced to endure quickened their senses. They began to think. A new light dawned upon their dark skies. They rubbed the age-long sleep from their eyes. They had long felt the brutalizing effect of class rule; now they saw the cause of it. Slowly but steadily they became class-conscious. They said, "We are brothers, we are comrades," and they saw themselves multiplied by millions. They caught the prophetic battle-cry of Karl Marx, the world's greatest labor leader, the inspired evangel of working-class emancipation, "Workers of all countries, unite!"

And now, behold! The international Socialist movement spreads out over all the nations of the earth. The world's workers are aroused at last. They are no longer on their knees; their bowed bodies are now erect. Despair has given way to hope, weakness to strength, fear to courage. They no longer cringe and supplicate; they hold up their heads and command. They have ceased to fear their masters and have learned to trust themselves.

And this is how the Socialist Party came to be born. It was quickened into life in the bitter struggle of the world's enslaved workers. It expresses their collective determination to break their fetters and emancipate themselves and the race. . . .

The appeal of the Socialist Party is to all the useful people of the nation, all who work with brain and muscle to produce the nation's wealth and who promote its progress and conserve its civilization.

Only they who bear its burdens may rightfully enjoy the blessings of civilized society.

There are no boundary lines to separate race from race, sex from sex or creed from creed in the Socialist Party. The common rights of all are equally recognized.

Every human being is entitled to sunlight and air, to what his labor produces, and to an equal chance with every other human being to unfold and ripen and give to the world the riches of his mind and soul. . . .

The infallible test of a political party is the private ownership of the sources of wealth and the means of life. Apply that test to the Republican, Democratic and Progressive parties and upon that basic, fundamental issue you will find them essentially one and the same. They differ according to the conflicting interests of the privileged classes, but at bottom they are alike and stand for capitalist class rule and working class slavery.

The new Progressive Party is a party of progressive capitalism. It is lavishly financed and shrewdly advertised. But it stands for the rule of capitalism all the same.

When the owners of the trusts finance a party to put themselves out of business; when they turn over their wealth to the people from whom they stole it and go to work for a living, it will be time enough to consider the merits of the Roosevelt Progressive Party.

One question is sufficient to determine the true status of all these parties. Do they want the workers to own the tools they work with, control their own jobs and secure to themselves the wealth they produce? Certainly not. That is utterly ridiculous and impossible from their point of view.

The Republican, Democratic and Progressive parties all stand for the private ownership by the capitalists of the productive machinery used by the workers, so that the capitalists can continue to filch the wealth produced by the workers.

The Socialist Party is the only party which declares that the tools of labor belong to labor and that the wealth produced by the working class belong to the working class. . . .

The solidarity of the working class is the salient force in the social transformation of which we behold the signs upon every hand. Nearer and nearer they are being drawn together in the bonds of unionism; clearer and clearer becomes their collective vision; greater and greater the power that throbs within them.

*   *   *

The capitalist class despise a working class party. Why should the working class give their support to a capitalist class party?

Capitalist misrule under which workingmen suffer slavery and the most galling injustice exists only because it has workingmen's support. Withdraw that support and capitalism is dead.

The capitalists can enslave and rob the workers only by the consent of the workers when they cast their ballots on election day.

Every vote cast for a capitalist party, whatever its name, is a vote for wage-slavery, for poverty and degradation.

Every vote cast for the Socialist Party, the workers' own party, is a vote for emancipation. . . .

Poverty, high prices, unemployment, child slavery, widespread misery and haggard want in a land bursting with abundance; prostitution and insanity, suicide and crime, these in solemn numbers tell the tragic story of capitalism's saturnalia of blood and tears and shame as its end draws near.

It is to abolish this monstrous system and the misery and crime which flow from it in a direful and threatening stream that the Socialist Party was organized and now makes its appeal to the intelligence and conscience of the people. Social reorganization is the imperative demand of this world-wide revolutionary movement.

The Socialist Party's mission is not only to destroy capitalist despotism but to establish industrial and social democracy. To this end the workers are steadily organizing and fitting themselves for the day when they shall take control of the people's industries and when the right to work shall be as inviolate as the right to breathe the breath of life. . . .

40

EUGENE V. DEBS

Opening Speech of the Campaign

August 10, 1912

This speech kicked off Debs's presidential campaign and was reprinted in the Socialist newspaper Appeal to Reason. *In opening his campaign, Debs argued that the Progressive movement was a futile attempt to adjust to changing economic conditions — particularly the rise of corporate capitalism. Only socialism, Debs believed, could truly appeal "to the allegiance and support of the workers and producers of the nation."*

... Parties but express in political terms the economic interests of those who compose them. This is the rule. The republican party represents the capitalist class, the democratic party the middle class, and the Socialist party the working class.

There is no fundamental difference between the republican and democratic parties. Their principles are identical. They are both capitalist parties and both stand for the capitalist system, and such differences as there are between them involve no principle but are the outgrowth of the conflicting interests of large and small capitalists.

The republican and democratic parties are alike threatened with destruction. Their day of usefulness is passed and they among them who see the handwriting on the wall and call themselves "progressives" and "insurgents" are struggling in vain to adjust these parties to the new conditions.

There is one infallible test that fixes the status of a political party and its candidates. Who finances them?

With this test applied to Theodore Roosevelt we have no trouble in locating him. He is above all "a practical man." He was practical in allowing the steel trust to raid the Tennessee Coal and Iron company; he was practical when he legalized the notorious "Alton Steal"; he was

Eugene V. Debs, "Debs' Opening Speech of the Campaign," *Appeal to Reason,* 871, August 10, 1912, 4.

practical when he had Harriman raise $340,000 for his campaign fund; and he is practical now in having the steel trust and the harvester trust, who made an anteroom of the white house when he was president, pour out their slush funds by millions to put him back in the white house and keep him there.

Taft and Roosevelt, and the republican party, of which they are the candidates, are all financed by the trusts, and is it necessary to add that the trusts also consist of practical men and that they do not finance a candidate or a party they do not control? . . .

Roosevelt must stand upon the record he made when he was president and had the power, and not upon his empty promises as a ranting demagogue and a vote-seeking politician.

For the very reason that the trusts are pouring out their millions to literally buy his nomination and election and force him into the white house for a third term, and if possible for life, the people should rise in their might and repudiate him as they never have repudiated a recreant official who betrayed them. . . .

The democratic party, like its republican ally, is a capitalist party, the only difference being that it represents the minor divisions of the capitalist class. It is true that there are some plutocrats and trust magnates in the democratic party but as a rule it is composed of the smaller capitalists who have been worsted by the larger ones and are now demanding that the trusts be destroyed and, in effect, that the laws of industrial evolution be suspended.

The democratic party, like the republican party, is financed by the capitalist class. Belmont, Ryan, Roger Sullivan, Taggart and Hinky Dink are liberal contributors to its fund. The Tammany organization in New York, notorious for its corruption and for its subservancy to the powers that rule capitalist society, is one of the controlling factors in the democratic party.

Woodrow Wilson is the candidate of the democratic party for president. He was seized upon as a "progressive"; as a man who would appeal to the common people, but he never could have been nominated without the votes controlled by Tammany and the "predatory interests" so fiercely denounced in the convention by William Jennings Bryan*. . . .

---

*William Jennings Bryan was a populist Democrat who spoke out for farmers and individuals and had run, and lost, three times as the Democratic presidential nominee.

* * *

The republican convention at Chicago and the democratic convention at Baltimore were composed of professional politicians, office-holders, office-seekers, capitalists, retainers, and swarms of parasites and mercenaries of all descriptions.

There were no working men in either convention. They were not fit to be there. All they are fit for is to march in the mud, yell themselves hoarse and ratify the choice of their masters on election day.

The working class was not represented in the republican convention at Chicago or the democratic convention at Baltimore. Those were the political conventions of the capitalist class and the few flattering platform phrases in reference to labor were incorporated for the sole purpose of catching the votes of the working class.

Let the American workers remember that they are not fit to sit as delegates in a republican or democratic national convention; that they are not fit to write a republican or democratic national platform; that all they are fit for is to elect the candidates of their masters to office so that when they go out on strike against starvation they may be shot dead in their tracks as the reward of their servility to their masters and their treason to themselves. . . .

In contrast with these important, corrupt and senile capitalist parties, without principles and without ideals, stands the virile young working class party, the international Socialist party of the world. The convention which nominated its candidates and wrote its platform at Indianapolis was a working class convention.

The Socialist party is the only party which honestly represents the working class in this campaign and the only party that has a moral right to appeal to the allegiance and suport of the workers and producers of the nation. . . .

The Socialist party being the political expression of the rising working class stands for the absolute overthrow of the existing capitalist system and for the reorganization of society into an industrial and social democracy.

This will mean an end to the private ownership of the means of life; it will mean an end to wage-slavery; it will mean an end to the army of the unemployed; it will mean an end to the poverty of the masses, the prostitution of womanhood, and the murder of childhood.

It will mean the beginning of a new era of civilization; the dawn of a happier day for the children of men. It will mean that this earth is for those who inhabit it and wealth for those who produce it. It will mean society organized upon a co-operative basis, collectively owning the sources of wealth and the means of production, and producing wealth to satisfy human wants and not to gorge a privileged few. It will mean that there shall be work for the workers and that all shall be workers, and it will also mean that there shall be leisure for the workers and that all shall enjoy it. It will mean that women shall be the comrades and equals of men, sharing with them on equal terms the opportunities as well as the responsibilities and the benefits as well as the burdens of civilized life. . . .

No longer can the workers be pitted against each other in capitalist parties by designing politicians to their mutual undoing. They have made the discovery that they have brains as well as hands, that they can think as well as work, and that they do not need politicians to advise them how to vote, nor masters to rob them of the fruits of their labor.

Slowly but surely there is being established the economic and political unity and solidarity of the workers of the world. The Socialist party is the political expression of that unity and solidarity.

41

SOCIALIST PARTY

Platform

May 25, 1912

The argument offered in the Socialist party platform in many ways paralleled the procorporate view. The Socialists agreed that corporations "improved methods in industry" and were more efficient (that is they "cheapen[ed] the cost of production"). However, they believed that economic inequities produced by the increasingly organized economy left owners with more wealth and workers with less. Consequently, they drew very different conclusions than Roosevelt and Van Hise, arguing that collective

---

"Platform Adopted at the Late National Socialist Convention," *Appeal to Reason,* 860, May 25, 1912, 2.

ownership, rather than government regulation of corporations, was the only solution. It is also important to note that economic and industrial solutions take precedence over political solutions in this platform.

The representatives of the Socialist party in national convention at Indianapolis declared that the capitalist system has outgrown its historical function, and has become utterly incapable of meeting the problems now confronting society. We denounce this outgrown system as incompetent and corrupt and the source of unspeakable misery and suffering to the whole working class. . . .

In spite of the multiplication of labor-saving machines and improved methods in industry which cheapen the cost of production, the share of the producers grows ever less, and the prices of all the necessities of life steadily increase. The boasted prosperity of this nation is for the owning class alone. To the rest it means only greater hardship and misery. The high cost of living is felt in every home. Millions of wage workers have seen the purchasing power of their wages decrease until life has become a desperate battle for mere existence. . . .

Society is divided into warring groups and classes, based upon material interests. Fundamentally, this struggle is a conflict between the two main classes, one of which, the capitalist class, owns the means of production, and the other, the working class, must use these means of production on terms dictated by the owners. . . .

As measures calculated to strengthen the working class in its fight for the realization of its ultimate aim, the Co-operative Commonwealth, and to increase its power of resistance against capitalist oppression, we advocate and pledge ourselves and our elected officers to the following program:

Collective Ownership

1. The collective ownership and democratic management of railroads, wire and wireless telegraphs and telephones, express services, steamboat lines and all other social means of transportation and communication and of all large-scale industries.
2. The immediate acquirement by the municipalities, the states or the federal government of all train elevators, stock yards, storage warehouses, and other distributing agencies, in order to reduce the present extortionate cost of living. . . .

Industrial Demands

The conservation of human resources, particularly of the lives and well-being of the workers and their families:

1. By shortening the workday in keeping with the increased productiveness of machinery.
2. By securing to every worker a rest period of not less than a day and a half in each week.
3. By securing a more effective inspection of workshops, factories and mines.
4. By forbidding the employment of children under sixteen years of age. . . .

Political Demands

1. The absolute freedom of press, speech, and assemblage.
2. The adoption of a graduated income tax, the increase of the rates of the present corporation tax and the extension of inheritance taxes, graduated in proportion to the value of the estate and to nearness of kin—the proceeds of these taxes to be employed in the socialization of industry.
3. The gradual reduction of all tariff duties, particularly those on the necessities of life. The government to guarantee the re-employment of wage earners who may be disemployed by reason of changes in tariff schedules.
4. The abolition of the monopoly ownership of patents and the substitution of collective ownership, with direct rewards to inventors by premiums or royalties.
5. Unrestricted and equal suffrage for men and women.
6. The adoption of the initiative, referendum and recall and of proportional representation, nationally as well as locally.
7. The abolition of the senate and of the veto power of the president.
8. The election of the president and the vice president by direct vote of the people.
9. The abolition of the power usurped by the supreme court of the United States to pass upon the constitutionality of the legislation enacted by congress. National laws to be repealed only by act of congress or by a referendum vote of the whole people. . . .

42

APPEAL TO REASON

Mr. Voter Beware . . .

November 2, 1912

Debs's belief that the three other parties promised reform only to win votes found expression in this cartoon. The cartoon draws a direct parallel between corporate development and capitalism, an argument Debs and the Socialists reiterated in most of their speeches in 1912.

Appeal to Reason, 883, November 2, 1912.

43

APPEAL TO REASON

The Woman Question
January 13, 1912
and
What Socialism Offers
September 28, 1912

Appeal to Reason *used the Socialists' support for women's rights, and especially women's suffrage, as a way to differentiate not only between capitalism and socialism, but between Debs and the other political candidates, none of whom had a long record of support for women's suffrage.*

The Woman Question

This is the question that is coming to the front because it can no longer remain in the background. It is no longer a mere demand for votes but an uprising on the part of intelligent women in behalf of their sex. They are breaking the fetters of the centuries and are at last coming to their own.

There is no reason why woman should be denied any human right. The very fact that she is a human being is all that is required to establish her right as a citizen and a voter, the equal of man in every respect whatsoever.

It is the glory of the Socialist movement, this despised proletarian uprising, that from its inception it championed the cause of woman, and in every battle it has fought it has stood uncompromisingly for equal rights without regard to sex.

There could be no social revolution with the women of the world denied their rightful place in it, and there never can be a free nation, a real democracy, in which woman is denied any right or privilege enjoyed by man.

We hail woman as our comrade and equal, and we rejoice in the fact that more and more she is realizing that the Socialist movement is

Appeal to Reason, 841, January 13, 1912, 1; *Appeal to Reason,* 878, September 28, 1912, 1.

her movement and is rallying to its standard in increasing numbers all over the civilized world.

What Socialism Offers

44

FRED D. WARREN

Letter to Eugene V. Debs

August 8, 1912

Fred Warren was the editor of Appeal to Reason *and a close friend of Debs'. He sent this letter after attending the Progressive party convention. Like many other observers, Warren noted the similarities between ideas expressed in Roosevelt's speech and socialist ideas.*

August 8, 1912 [Girard, Kansas]

Dear Gene:

. . . I attended the Roosevelt convention in Chicago. I am impressed with the importance of the 3rd party move. There is something strikingly

Fred D. Warren, letter to Eugene V. Debs, in *Letters of Eugene V. Debs,* vol. 2, ed. J. Robert Constantine (Urbana: University of Illinois Press, 1990), 533–36.

significant in the gathering together of 14,000 men and women from
all parts of the nation to declare that they no longer were republicans,
thus severing the political ties of a life time. I sat within twenty feet of
Roosevelt and there were times when I could have shut my eyes and
readily believed that I was listening to a Socialist soap boxer! In the
decorations, red predominated and the red bandana was very much in
evidence. My prediction that Roosevelt would steal our platform bodily
has been fulfilled. I am also firmly convinced that he is to be the central figure around which the campaign will be waged this year. His slo-
gan will be that the nation must elect him in order to save the people
from Socialism on one hand and predatory wealth on the other. Many
of our half baked converts will join in the hue and cry that it is better
to have a half loaf than none at all and they will be fooled by his false
promises. This movement of Roosevelt's will be helped by the differences in our own ranks. It is therefore the duty of every loyal Socialist
at this crisis to lay aside petty differences and stand shoulder to shoulder with its comrades who are fighting the real battle for the emancipation of the working class. This is what I am resolved to do and no
amount of threats or persuasion will ever again lead me to depart from
that policy. . . .

Sincerely yours,
[Fred D. Warren]

45

CHICAGO WORLD

Eugene V. Debs Says Moose Party
Stole Socialist Planks

August 15, 1912

and

APPEAL TO REASON

The Acid Test

September 21, 1912

After receiving Warren's letter from the Progressive party convention, Debs publicly charged Roosevelt with adopting the Socialist program himself. Debs believed, however, that in arguing for a government commission to regulate corporate behavior rather than collective ownership of trusts and corporations, Roosevelt stripped the Socialist program of its power. Debs's argument found visual form in a cartoon that Appeal to Reason *ran a few weeks later. For a comparison with Roosevelt's ideas, see "A Confession of Faith" (Document 7).*

Eugene V. Debs Says Moose Party Stole Socialist Planks

The *New York World* and the *New York Times* both wired Candidate Debs yesterday asking him for an expression regarding the Roosevelt platform. . . .

To the *World,* Debs wired the following answer:

"Editor of the World, *New York City:*
"The platform of the Roosevelt Progressive party has much in it with which Socialists are in full agreement but it does not contain

---

"Eugene V. Debs Says Moose Party Stole Socialist Planks," *Chicago World,* August 15, 1912, in *Papers of Eugene V. Debs* (microfilm edition), reel 17; *Appeal to Reason,* 877, September 21, 1912, 4.

any of the vital and fundamental principles of Socialism and is [in] no sense a Socialist platform. It may perhaps be best described as a platform of progressive capitalism. Its declarations aim at some of the flagrant evils and abuses of capitalism, while the platform as a whole supports and strengthens the existing system, and, doubtless, has the full approval of the steel trust and harvester trust, and like interests which financed Roosevelt's campaign for the nomination, and are now financing the campaign of his Progressive party. . . .

"Mr. Roosevelt now stands upon a platform of his own making, which advocates doctrines which but a few years ago he denounced as anarchy and treason, and if he succeeds in convincing the American people of his sincerity and good faith, the trusts will have made no mistake in picking him for a life tenure in the White House."

. . . The inquiry of the *New York Times* elicited the following in reply:

"Editor New York Times, *New York City:*
"The most significant thing about the Roosevelt Progressive convention is that it represented hundreds of thousands of men who have voted the Republican ticket all their lives, and who have now quit the Republican party forever. The progressive tendency here manifested can never be checked, but will become more and more pronounced until it finds expression in Socialism. . . .

"The really progressive planks in the Progressive platform were taken bodily from the Socialist platform and even the red flag of Socialism was appropriated, or at least imitated, by the red bandana of the Roosevelt followers.

"As the leader of the Bull Moose party, Mr. Roosevelt must be judged by his performances and not by his pledges. He was President almost eight years and how he dealt with the trust evil is well known to the country. It is especially well known to the trusts themselves who financed his campaign for the nomination and are now financing the campaign for his election.

"The Progressive party as a party is not only not progressive, but it is reactionary. In the aggregate it is a middle class protest against trust domination. The middle class will furnish . . . [the] votes, and the trusts in the event of Roosevelt's election, will take care of the administration. . . ."

The Acid Test

*Working in the "political laboratory," this laborer applies "Marxian Socialist Aid" to "Roosevelt's Socialist Jewels." Paste is a combination of minerals heated and fused to make fake precious gemstones. Some acids will break down "paste," or fake gems, whereas real stones remain intact. The statement "it's just paste" suggests that Roosevelt's platform was a fake version of the "real" and valuable Socialist platform.

A 1912 Election Chronology
(1877–1930)

1877

July: Nationwide railroad strikes. State and federal troops are called out in Baltimore, Md., Martinsburg, W. Va., Pittsburgh, Pa., and other cities to suppress strikers.

1879

Henry George publishes *Progress and Poverty.*

1887

Congress creates Interstate Commerce Commission.

1889

September 18: Hull House settlement house opens in Chicago.

December: Andrew Carnegie publishes essay "Wealth" (later retitled "The Gospel of Wealth"), calling for the rich to spend excess earnings on philanthropy.

1890

Congress passes Sherman Antitrust Act.

1892

November: Populism reaches high point nationally as Populist presidential candidate James Weaver receives more than 1 million votes.

1893

January–April: Twenty-eight banks suspend payments, beginning Depression of 1893.

1894

June–July: Pullman strike involving American railway union freezes America's railroads, leading to federal intervention against strikers.

1895

September 18: Booker T. Washington delivers Atlanta Exposition address, accepting social separation between blacks and whites in the South.

1896

In *Plessy v. Ferguson,* U.S. Supreme Court declares laws requiring segregation and separate facilities for blacks and whites are legal.

1897

Merger movement begins with ten industrial mergers.

1898

In *Williams v. Mississippi,* U.S. Supreme Court upholds constitutionality of disfranchisement clauses in southern state constitutions.

Merger movement increases to twenty-eight industrial mergers.

1899

Merger movement reaches height of 106 business consolidations.

1900

American Tobacco Company produces roughly one-half of tobacco purchased in United States.

Decline in business mergers to 42.

1900–1914

On average 1 million immigrants enter the United States each year.

1901

September: President William McKinley assassinated. Theodore Roosevelt becomes president.

United States Steel is formed from two hundred separate companies.

Business mergers hold steady at forty-eight.

1902

October: Roosevelt mediates between mine operators and United Mine Workers to force settlement in anthracite coal strike.

1904

March 14: Roosevelt's Justice Department achieves notable antitrust victory in Northern Securities case.

November: Roosevelt elected president. Pledges not to run again.

November: Wisconsin voters institute direct primary elections for political nominations.

McClure's Magazine prints Ida W. Tarbell's *The History of Standard Oil,* detailing the build-up of Standard Oil's monopolistic control of oil refining.

Height of merger movement; 318 firms control 40 percent of U.S. industrial output.

1905

June: Industrial Workers of the World (IWW, or "Wobblies") formed.

1906

March: Cosmopolitan magazine publishes David Graham Phillips's "The Treason of the Senate."

1908

November: William Howard Taft elected president by defeating William Jennings Bryan (Democrat) and Socialist party candidate Eugene V. Debs, who gains national attention (and 420,000 votes) by campaigning across the country in the "Red Special" train.

1909

August 5: Taft signs Payne-Aldrich Tariff into law, angering Republican reformers.

September 17: Taft, in a speech at Winona, Minnesota, defends new tariff as "best tariff" ever passed, embittering reformers in his party.

1910

January 7: Taft fires Chief Forester Gifford Pinchot, triggering Ballinger-Pinchot affair.

June 16: Roosevelt returns to United States from African safari.

August 31: Roosevelt begins national speaking tour with "New Nationalism" speech at Osawatomie, Kansas.

November: Midterm congressional elections result in victories for Democrats and anti-Taft Republicans.

Woodrow Wilson elected Governor of New Jersey.

December: National Progressive Republican League formed to challenge Taft for 1912 Republican presidential nomination.

1911

Frederick Winslow Taylor publishes *Principles of Scientific Management.*

March 25, 1911: Fire in Triangle Shirt Waist factory results in deaths of 146 workers.

May: In Standard Oil and American Tobacco cases, Supreme Court develops "rule of reason," limiting application of Sherman Antitrust Act.

June: Socialist newspaper *Appeal to Reason* reaches circulation of more than 500,000 copies.

October 26: Taft's Attorney General begins antitrust prosecution against United States Steel.

1912

Charles Van Hise publishes *Concentration and Control.*

February 2: La Follette gives disastrous speech at Philadelphia publishers banquet and is rumored to have had mental breakdown.

February 21: Roosevelt delivers "A Charter of Democracy" speech to Ohio constitutional convention.

February 24: Roosevelt declares himself candidate for Republican presidential nomination.

March 16: America's first presidential primary held in North Dakota.

April 19: Federal children's bureau created.

June 18: Republican party Committee on Credentials rules against Roosevelt.

June 22: Roosevelt and followers "bolt" from Republican party; Taft nominated as Republican candidate for presidency.

July 2: Democratic party nominates Wilson for presidency.

August 6: Roosevelt accepts Progressive party presidential nomination at Progressive party's first national convention.

August 28: Brandeis and Wilson meet for the first time.

September: Brandeis publishes "Trusts, Efficiency and the New Party," critiquing Roosevelt's economic program, in *Collier's Magazine.*

October 14: An assassin shoots Roosevelt in Milwaukee, Wisconsin.

1913

March 3: More than 5,000 women march in women's suffrage parade in Washington, D.C.

March 4: Woodrow Wilson sworn in as president.

April: Seventeenth Amendment ratified, making federal income tax constitutional.

October 3: Underwood-Simmons Tariff law enacted; lowers tariffs as a whole.

December 23: Federal Reserve Act (creating new American banking system) becomes law.

1914

September 26: Federal Trade Commission Act becomes law.

October 15: Clayton Antitrust Act becomes law.

1916

November: Wilson reelected president over Republican candidate Charles Evans Hughes.

1919

January 6: Roosevelt dies in Oyster Bay, New York.

1920

August 18: Nineteenth Amendment ratified, assuring women's right to vote.

1924

February 3: Wilson dies in Washington, D.C.

1926

October 20: Eugene Debs dies in Terre Haute, Indiana.

1930

March 8: Taft dies in Washington, D.C.

Questions for Consideration

1. Could any of the programs that the politicians and advisers proposed in 1912 have been advanced without the existence of their opponents' ideas? To what extent did each politician's ideas develop through dialogue or debate with their opponents?

2. Historians have found it difficult to identify a single idea that was common to all forms of Progressivism. Was there a common or unifying feature to the campaign of 1912?

3. In 1912 Eugene Debs charged Theodore Roosevelt with stealing the Socialists' ideas. Was the New Nationalism a watered-down version of socialism, or did Roosevelt draw different conclusions from the same assumptions that Debs started with? Was Progressivism an American adaptation of socialism?

4. Did Woodrow Wilson's ideas develop during the 1912 presidential campaign?

5. To what extent do the different arguments in this volume reflect conflicting sets of social, economic, and political values? Do these values continue to shape the society that you live in?

6. Taft spent much of 1912 trying to counter the impression that he was antidemocratic. Was this impression accurate? Could Taft be said to have been working from a different, but still legitimate, definition of democracy? To what extent were the arguments in 1912 a reflection of a number of competing visions of democracy?

7. What did the people you have read about in this book mean by the term "efficient"? When procorporationists such as Charles Van Hise or Roosevelt argued that corporations were valuable because they produced efficiently, what cultural value were they emphasizing?

8. After Roosevelt left the Republican convention, Wilson simply needed to not make any egregious mistakes in order to win the 1912 election. Despite this almost foregone conclusion, the 1912 election was tremendously important. Why, aside from determining who will serve as president, are national elections important in American society?

9. In 1911 La Follette, Brandeis, and Van Hise had dinner together and discussed the economic problems facing the nation. Imagine that Taft, Roosevelt, Debs, and Wilson had all shown up as well. Write a dialogue among the many different participants in the 1912 election.

10. Your class may want to conduct a debate among the four major contenders in 1912. Think about what each figure would want to emphasize if he had five minutes to address the nation as a whole. What questions might the candidates want to ask one another? Developing probing questions can help reveal a great deal about the assumptions and ideas behind each program.

Selected Bibliography

THE PROGRESSIVE ERA

General Works

Buenker, John D., John C. Burnham, and Robert M. Crunden. *Progressivism*. Cambridge, Mass.: Schenkman, 1977.

———. *The Progressive Era, 1893–1914.* Vol. 4 of *The History of Wisconsin,* edited by William Fletcher Thompson. Madison: State Historical Society of Wisconsin, 1998.

Campbell, Ballard C., ed. *The Human Tradition in the Gilded Age and Progressive Era.* Wilmington, Del.: SR Books, 2000.

Diner, Steven J. *A Very Different Age: Americans of the Progressive Era.* New York: Hill & Wang, 1998.

Eisenach, Eldon J. *The Lost Promise of Progressivism.* Lawrence: University Press of Kansas, 1994.

Gould, Lewis, ed. *The Progressive Era.* Syracuse: Syracuse University Press, 1974.

Hays, Samuel. *The Response to Industrialism: 1885–1914.* Chicago: University of Chicago Press, 1957.

Hofstadter, Richard. *The Age of Reform: From Bryan to FDR.* New York: Vintage Books, 1955.

Link, Arthur S., and Richard L. McCormick. *Progressivism.* Arlington Heights, Ill.: Harlan Davidson, Inc., 1983.

Milkis, Sidney M., and Jerome Mileur, eds. *Progressivism and the New Democracy.* Amherst: University of Massachusetts Press, 1999.

Painter, Nell Irvin. *Standing at Armageddon: The United States, 1877–1919.* New York: W. W. Norton & Co., 1987.

Rodgers, Daniel T. "In Search of Progressivism." *Reviews in American History* 20, no. 4 (Dec. 1982): 113–32.

Wiebe, Robert H. *The Search for Order, 1877–1920.* New York: Hill & Wang, 1967.

Economics/Political Economy

Berk, Gerald. *Alternative Tracks: The Constitution of American Industrial Order, 1865–1917*. Baltimore: Johns Hopkins University Press, 1994.

Bringhurst, Bruce. *Antitrust and the Oil Monopoly: The Standard Oil Cases, 1890–1911*. Westport, Conn.: Greenwood Press, 1979.

Chandler, Alfred D. *The Visible Hand: The Managerial Revolution in American Business*. Cambridge, Mass.: Harvard University Press, 1977.

Galambos, Louis. *The Public Image of Big Business in America, 1880–1940*. Baltimore: Johns Hopkins University Press, 1975.

Keller, Morton. *Regulating a New Economy: Public Policy and Economic Change in America, 1900–1933*. Cambridge, Mass.: Harvard University Press, 1990.

Kolko, Gabriel. *Railroads and Regulation, 1877–1916*. Princeton, N.J.: Princeton University Press, 1965.

Lamoreaux, Naomi R. *The Great Merger Movement in American Business, 1895–1904*. New York: Cambridge University Press, 1985.

Livingston, James. *Pragmatism and the Political Economy of Cultural Revolution, 1850–1940*. Chapel Hill: University of North Carolina Press, 1994.

Sklar, Martin J. *The Corporate Reconstruction of American Capitalism, 1890–1916: The Market, the Law, and Politics*. New York: Cambridge University Press, 1988.

Taussig, Frank W. *The Tariff History of the United States*. 8th ed. New York: G. P. Putnam's Sons, 1931. Reprint. New York: Johnson Reprint Corp., 1966.

Van Hise, Charles R. *Concentration and Control: A Solution of the Trust Problem in the United States*. New York: Macmillan Co., 1912.

Weinstein, James. *The Corporate Ideal in the Liberal State: 1900–1918*. Boston: Beacon Press, 1968.

Wolman, Paul. *Most Favored Nation: The Republican Revisionists and U.S. Tariff Policy, 1897–1912*. Chapel Hill: University of North Carolina Press.

Politics

Broderick, Francis L. *Progressivism at Risk: Electing a President in 1912*. New York: Greenwood Press, 1989.

Buenker, John D. *Urban Liberalism and Progressive Reform*. New York: Charles Scribner's Sons, 1973.

Cherny, Robert W. *Populism, Progressivism, and the Transformation of Nebraska Politics, 1885–1915*. Lincoln: University of Nebraska Press, 1981.

Croly, Herbert. *The Promise of American Life*. New York: Capricorn Press, 1964. Reprint, Boston: Northeastern University Press, 1989.

Flexner, Eleanor, and Ellen Fitzpatrick. *Century of Struggle: The Woman's Rights Movement in the United States.* Enlarged edition. Cambridge: Harvard University Press, 1996.

Gilmore, Glenda Elizabeth. *Gender and Jim Crow: Women and the Politics of White Supremacy in North Carolina, 1896–1920.* Chapel Hill: University of North Carolina Press, 1996.

Holt, James. *Congressional Insurgents and the Party System, 1909–1916.* Cambridge, Mass.: Harvard University Press, 1967.

Kelly, Frank K. *The Fight for the White House: The Story of 1912.* New York: Crowell, 1961.

Kolko, Gabriel. *The Triumph of Conservatism: A Reinterpretation of American History, 1900–1916.* New York: Free Press of Glencoe, 1963.

Kraditor, Aileen S. *The Ideas of the Woman Suffrage Movement, 1890–1920.* Garden City, N.Y.: Anchor Books, 1971.

Lippmann, Walter. *Drift and Mastery.* Revised introduction and notes by William E. Leuchtenburg. Englewood Cliffs, N.J.: Prentice-Hall Inc., 1961. Reprint. Madison: University of Wisconsin Press, 1985.

McCormick, Richard L. *The Party Period and Public Policy: American Politics from the Age of Jackson to the Progressive Era.* New York: Oxford University Press, 1986.

McGerr, Michael E. *The Decline of Popular Politics: The American North, 1865–1928.* New York: Oxford University Press, 1986.

Mowry, George E. *Theodore Roosevelt and the Progressive Movement.* Madison: University of Wisconsin, 1946. Reprint, New York: Hill & Wang, 1960.

———. *The Era of Theodore Roosevelt and the Birth of Modern America.* New York: Harper & Row, 1958.

Penick, James L. *Progressive Politics and Conservation: The Ballinger-Pinchot Affair.* Chicago: University of Chicago Press, 1968.

Sanders, Elizabeth. *Roots of Reform: Farmers, Workers, and the American State: 1877–1917.* Chicago: University of Chicago Press, 1999.

Skowronek, Stephen. *Building a New American State: The Expansion of National Administrative Capacities, 1877–1920.* New York: Cambridge University Press, 1982.

Social Policy/Social Reform

Addams, Jane. *Twenty Years at Hull-House.* Edited by Victoria Bissell Brown. Boston: Bedford/St. Martin's, 1999.

Crunden, Robert Morse. *Ministers of Reform: The Progressives' Achievement in American Civilization, 1889–1920.* New York: Basic Books, 1982.

Davis, Allen Freeman. *Spearheads for Reform: The Social Settlements and the Progressive Movement, 1890–1914.* New York: Oxford University Press, 1967.

Dawley, Alan. *Struggles for Justice: Social Responsibility and the Liberal State*. Cambridge, Mass.: Harvard University Press, 1991.

Kloppenberg, James T. *Uncertain Victory: Social Democracy and Progressivism in European and American Thought, 1870–1920*. New York: Oxford University Press, 1986.

Muncy, Robyn. *Creating a Female Dominion in American Reform, 1890–1935*. New York: Oxford University Press, 1991.

Rodgers, Daniel T. *Atlantic Crossings: Social Politics in a Progressive Age*. Cambridge, Mass.: Harvard University Press, 1998.

Skocpol, Theda. *Protecting Soldiers and Mothers: The Political Origins of Social Policy in the United States*. Cambridge, Mass.: Harvard University Press, 1992.

Thelen, David P. *The New Citizenship: The Origins of Progressivism in Wisconsin, 1885–1900*. Columbia: University of Missouri Press, 1972.

Multimedia Sources

In Their Own Words: The U.S. Presidential Elections of 1908 and 1912. Marston Records, 2000.

1912: Competing Visions for America. Web page available at http://1912.history.ohio-state.edu/default.htm.

THE PARTICIPANTS

Louis Brandeis

Brandeis, Louis D. *Other People's Money and How the Bankers Use It*. Edited by Melvin I. Urofsky. Boston: Bedford/St. Martin's, 1995.

McCraw, Thomas K. *Prophets of Regulation: Charles Francis Adams, Louis D. Brandeis, James M. Landis, Alfred E. Kahn*. Cambridge, Mass.: Harvard University Press, 1984.

Mason, Alpheus T. *Brandeis: A Free Man's Life*. New York: Viking Press, 1946.

Strum, Philippa. *Louis D. Brandeis: Justice of the People*. Cambridge, Mass.: Harvard University Press, 1984.

Urofsky, Melvin I. *Louis D. Brandeis and the Progressive Tradition*. Boston: Little, Brown, and Co., 1981.

Eugene V. Debs

Letters of Eugene V. Debs. Vol. 1, *1874–1912*. Edited by J. Robert Constantine. Urbana: University of Illinois Press, 1990.

The Papers of Eugene V. Debs. Sanford, N.C.: Microfilming Corporation of America, 1982. Microfilm.

Writings and Speeches of Eugene V. Debs. Introduction by Arthur Schlesinger Jr. New York: Hermitage Press, 1948.

Salvatore, Nick. *Eugene V. Debs: Citizen and Socialist*. Urbana: University of Illinois Press, 1982.

Robert La Follette

La Follette, Robert M. *La Follette's Autobiography: A Personal Narrative of Political Experiences.* Madison, Wis.: Robert M. La Follette Co., 1911.

Thelen, David P. *Robert M. La Follette and the Insurgent Spirit.* Boston: Little, Brown, and Co., 1976.

Unger, Nancy. *Fighting Bob La Follette: The Righteous Reformer.* Chapel Hill: University of North Carolina Press, 2000.

Theodore Roosevelt

Blum, John Morton. *The Republican Roosevelt.* 2nd ed. Cambridge, Mass.: Harvard University Press, 1977.

Cooper, John Milton Jr. *The Warrior and the Priest: Woodrow Wilson and Theodore Roosevelt.* Cambridge, Mass.: Harvard University Press, 1983.

Gould, Lewis. *The Presidency of Theodore Roosevelt.* Lawrence: University Press of Kansas, 1991.

Morris, Edmund. *The Rise of Theodore Roosevelt.* New York: Ballantine Books, 1980.

Roosevelt, Theodore. *An Autobiography.* New York: The Macmillan Co., 1913.

――――. *The Works of Theodore Roosevelt.* Vol. 17, *Social Justice and Popular Rule.* Edited by Hermann Hagedorn. New York: Charles Scribner's Sons, 1926.

――――. *The Letters of Theodore Roosevelt.* Vol. 7, *The Days of Armageddon.* Edited by Elting E. Morrison. Cambridge, Mass.: Harvard University Press, 1954.

――――. *The New Nationalism.* Introduction by William E. Leuchtenburg. Englewood Cliffs, N.J.: Prentice Hall, Inc., 1961. Reprint, Gloucester, Mass.: Peter Smith, 1971.

William Howard Taft

Anderson, Judith Icke. *William Howard Taft: An Intimate History.* New York: W. W. Norton & Co., 1981.

Coletta, Paolo. *The Presidency of William Howard Taft.* Lawrence: University Press of Kansas, 1973.

Pringle, Henry F. *The Life and Times of William Howard Taft: A Biography.* New York: Farrar & Rinehart, Inc., 1939.

Taft, William H. *Papers: 1890–1930.* Washington, D.C.: Library of Congress, 1969. Microfilm.

Woodrow Wilson

Clements, Kendrick A. *The Presidency of Woodrow Wilson.* Lawrence: University of Kansas Press, 1992.

George, Alexander L., and Juliette L. George. *Woodrow Wilson and Colonel House: A Personality Study.* n.p. John Day Co., 1956. Reprint, New York: Dover Publications Inc., 1964.

Heckscher, August. *Woodrow Wilson.* New York: Scribners, 1991.

Link, Arthur S. *Wilson: The Road to the White House.* Princeton, N.J.: Princeton University Press, 1947.

———. *Woodrow Wilson and the Progressive Era, 1900–1917.* New York: Harper & Brothers, 1954.

———. *Wilson: The New Freedom.* Princeton, N.J.: Princeton University Press, 1956.

———. *The Papers of Woodrow Wilson.* Vol. 24–25. Edited by Arthur S. Link. Princeton, N.J.: Princeton University Press, 1978.

Acknowledgments

Louis D. Brandeis, letters to Norman Hapgood, Alfred Brandeis, Arthur Norman Holcombe. Reprinted by permission from *Letters of Louis D. Brandeis: Vol. 2* by Melvin I. Urofsky and David W. Levy, eds., the State University of New York Press. © 1978, State University of New York. All rights reserved.

Theodore Roosevelt, letters to Theodore Roosevelt Jr., Benjamin Barr Lindsay, Chase Salmon Osborn, Mary Ella Lyon Swift, Florence Kelley, Jane Addams, Julian La Rose Harris. Reprinted by permission of the publisher from *The Letters of Theodore Roosevelt*, selected and edited by Elting E. Morison, Cambridge, Mass.: Harvard University Press. Copyright © 1954 by the President and Fellows of Harvard College.

Oswald Garrison Villard, diary excerpt. From Arthur S. Link, ed., *The Papers of Woodrow Wilson*. Copyright © 1987 by Princeton University Press. Reprinted by permission of Princeton University Press.

Woodrow Wilson, speech at Buffalo, New York. From Arthur S. Link, ed., *The Papers of Woodrow Wilson*. Copyright © 1987 by Princeton University Press. Reprinted by permission of Princeton University Press.

Woodrow Wilson and Louis D. Brandeis, correspondence. From Arthur S. Link, ed., *The Papers of Woodrow Wilson*. Copyright © 1987 by Princeton University Press. Reprinted by permission of Princeton University Press.

Index

195